# Developing Classroom Materials for Less Commonly Taught Languages

Bill Johnston
*with* Louis Janus

CENTER FOR ADVANCED RESEARCH
ON LANGUAGE ACQUISITION

*Office of International Programs*

## UNIVERSITY OF MINNESOTA

Center for Advanced Research on Language Acquisition
Working Paper

# Developing Classroom Materials for Less Commonly Taught Languages

First Edition, First Printing
Printed in the United States of America

Produced by

Center for Advanced Research on Language Acquisition
University of Minnesota
619 Heller Hall
271 19th Avenue South
Minneapolis, MN  55455
USA
612-626-8600
carla@umn.edu
http://www.carla.umn.edu

Desktop Publishing: Suzanne Hay
Cover Design: Aaron Shekey

This book was developed with significant support from the U.S. Department of Education, Office of Postsecondary Education, International Education Programs Service, Language Resource Center grant no. P229A020011. The contents of this publication do not necessarily reflect the positions or policies of the U.S. Department of Education.

---

Johnston, B. (with Janus, L.). (2007). *Developing classroom materials for less commonly taught languages.* (CARLA Working Paper Series). Minneapolis, MN: University of Minnesota, The Center for Advanced Research on Language Acquisition.

ISBN: 0-9722545-6-0

# Acknowledgments

My biggest debt is to the wonderful teachers who have taken the workshop in developing materials for LCTLs that Louis Janus and I have offered each summer since 1999 for the Center for Advanced Research on Language Acquisition, a Title VI National Language Resource Center at the University of Minnesota. Thanks to all of you, and double thanks to those whose materials are included in this book. Second, my thanks go to Louis Janus, who has been a joy to work with. I also thank Elaine Tarone and Karin Larson of CARLA for their support, encouragement, and patience, and to Suzanne Hay for her thorough work on the manuscript. My thanks go to my mentors in materials development—especially John Morgan and Ramon Shindler—for pointing the way. And lastly, I owe an eternal debt to my colleagues at Wrocław University in Poland in 1987-1991—Bartek Madejski, Magda Zamorska, Marian Zamorski, Ania Hałucha, Marzenna Gwoździńska, Tom Randolph, and the late great Krzyś Ordowski—who showed me that everything is possible. This book is for them.

# Copyright Permission

In a book devoted to using authentic materials it is critical to use as many actual authentic materials as possible, but getting permission to do so is not always straightforward, especially for the less commonly taught languages. Bill Johnston and Louis Janus, along with the Center for Advanced Research on Language Acquisition (CARLA), gratefully acknowledge those who have given their consent to reproduce the following extracts of copyrighted material.

"The Loving Dexterity" by William Carlos Willams is reprinted by permission of New Directions Publishing Corp. Full citation:
>   Williams, W. C. (1962). *Collected poems 1939-1962, Vol. II.* New York: New Directions Publishing Corp.

"Aunt Cecylia's Adventure" is reprinted with the permission of Bill Johnston who owns the copyright to the English translation of *The Shadow Catcher.* Full citation:
>   Szczypiorski, A. (1997). *The shadow catcher* (B. Johnston, Trans.). New York: Grove Press.

The lyrics of *Biyahe Tayo!* by Rene Nieva are reprinted with permission from Melo Villareal, owner and publisher of LakbayPilipinas.com.

The *Sears Tower Skydeck* brochure text is reprinted with permission from Carey Randall of Sears Tower Skydeck.

Extracts from the *Japanese Guide to Minnesota* are reprinted with permission from Greenspring Media.

The English translation of the poem "Speak" by Faiz Ahmed Faiz is reprinted with permission from Azfar Hussain, the poem's translator. Full citation:
>   Faiz, F. A., (1999). *Speak.* In P. Brians, M. Gallwey, D. Hughes, A. Hussain, R. Law, M. Myers, M. Neville, R. Schlesinger, A. Spitzer, & S. Swan (Eds.), *Reading about the world: Vol. 1* (3rd ed.). New York: Harcourt Brace.

The poem "A Martian Sends a Postcard Home" by Craig Raine is reprinted with permission from David Godwin Associates. Full citation:
>   Raine, C. (1980). *A Martian sends a postcard home.* Oxford: Oxford University Press.

The poem "Vacations in Kurpieland" by Anna Swir (Anna Świrszczyńska), translated by Czesław Miłosz and Leonard Nathan, is reprinted with permission from Copper Canyon Press. Full citation:
>   Swir, A. (1996) *Talking to my body.* (C. Miłosz & L. Nathan, Trans.) Port Townsend, WA: Copper Canyon Press.

The poem "Love Compared" by Nizar Kabbani is reprinted with permission from Interlink Publishing Group. Full citation:
>   Kabbani, N. (1998). *On entering the sea: The erotic and other poetry of Nizar Qabbani.* Northampton, MA: Interlink Publishing Group.

The lyrics of the song "Amsterdam" by Jacques Brel are reprinted with permission from Alfred Publishing under license agreement #1044774. Full citation as requested by copyright holder is as follows:

    *Amsterdam*. English Lyrics by Mort Shuman, Music by Jacques Brel.
    © 1968 (Renewed) Pouchenel, Editions & Mort Shuman Songs.
    All Rights on Behalf of Pouchenel, Editions Administered by Unichappell Music Inc.
    All Rights on Behalf of Mort Shuman Songs Administered by Warner-Tamerlane Publishing Corp.
    All Rights Reserved. Used by Permission of Alfred Publishing Co. Inc.

Extracts from *Uzbek: An Elementary Textbook* by Nigora Azimova are reprinted with permission from the Center for Languages of the Central Asian Region (CeLCAR) at Indiana University. Full citation:

    Azimova, N. (2006). *Uzbek: An elementary textbook*. Bloomington, IN: Indiana University, The
        Center for Languages of the Central Asian Region.

Extracts from the 2004 film *Vinci* are used with the permission of its director/screenwriter, Juliusz Machulski.

The comic strip *Welcome to Falling Rock National Park* is used with the permission of its author Josh Shalek.

TrackStar screen shots are used with the permission of Erica Schaapveld, 4Teachers Project Coordinator.

"Ukas lydklipp" screen shot is used with the permission of Nancy Aarsvold, St. Olaf College.

Makers cloze exercise and a Hot Potatoes listening activity screen shots were created by Louis Janus to illustrate use of these tools.

The graphic entitled "They" is used courtesy of the Department of Foreign Languages and Literatures, Purdue University. This project is supported by Center for Technology Enhanced Language Learning.

The graphic entitled "Under" is used courtesy of the University of Victoria's Language Teaching Clipart Library.

Every effort has been made to trace the owners of copyright material in this book, but we welcome contact from any copyright holder whom we have been unable to contact. If notified, CARLA will be pleased to rectify any error or omission at the earliest opportunity.

We also wish to thank the many teachers who have contributed materials developed during various instantiations of our summer institute on Developing Materials for Less Commonly Taught Languages held at CARLA. Their work adds to the richness of this volume and celebrates the creativity that is abundant within the LCTL teaching community:

Blaine Auer for "Speak," Valerie Borey for "The Sami," Imelda Gasmen for "Halika, Biyahe Tayo!", Andrea Gregg for "Sulunatuuq," Miaki Habuka for "What to Do in Minnesota," Ji-Eun Kim for "How to Perform Yoga," Leonora Kivuva for "Beauty," Phuong Nguyen for "Folk Song," Aeni Palsapah, Herlina Surbakti and Christine Sutandi-Sustano for "Making Gado-Gado," Samiha Salib for "Love Compared," Elyse Carter Vosen for "When Bear was Hungry," and Hanna Zmijewska-Emerson for "A Doll's House."

Last but not least, thanks to Kasia Rydel-Johnston for the use of several of her photographs.

# About the Authors

## Bill Johnston

After studying French and Russian at Oxford University, Bill Johnston taught English in Poland for several years. He completed his doctorate in Second Language Acquisition from the University of Hawai'i. Since then he has taught at the University of Minnesota and currently at Indiana University, where he is Associate Professor of Second Language Studies.

*Bill Johnston & Louis Janus*

Professor Johnston conducts research in language teacher education and teacher development, and in the moral dimensions of teaching. He is the author of *Values in English Language Teaching* (Lawrence Erlbaum, 2003) among numerous publications. In addition to his research, Professor Johnston frequently conducts workshops with teachers of LCTLs (Less Commonly Taught Languages). Since 1999 he has taught a summer institute on Developing Materials for LCTLs for the Center for Advanced Research on Language Acquisition (CARLA) at the University for Minnesota.

As a translator of Polish literature, Bill Johnston has fifteen books currently in print. Since coming to the U.S. he has remained active in promoting Polish culture, and is currently Director of Indiana University's Polish Studies Center.

## Louis Janus

Louis Janus is the coordinator of the Less Commonly Taught Languages (LCTL) Project at CARLA at the University of Minnesota. He oversees the database that lists where LCTLs are taught in North American schools from elementary to universities, study abroad and distance education settings, and manages the mailing lists the LCTL project sponsors. The LCTL project promotes good teaching and learning opportunities for LCTLs. He also develops material for the Virtual Picture Album and Virtual Audio Video Archives.

Janus holds the Ph.D. degree in Germanic Philology from the University of Minnesota. In addition to his work at CARLA, Janus has been an active teacher of Norwegian language and Scandinavian linguistics at the University of Minnesota and St. Olaf College. He is currently the president of the Norwegian Researchers and Teachers Association of North America. He developed and taught a graduate course on the Scandinavian Languages for reading knowledge. This course has been taught at the University of Minnesota and was most recently taught in Summer 2003 as an online course.

Janus has authored a grammar book, tapes, software for learning Norwegian, and was co-author of the lesson-a-day NorWord mailing list. In Spring 2000, Janus was the program leader at the Oslo Year Program at the University of Oslo. He is now writing a multimedia learners' dictionary for English speakers who are learning Norwegian.

# Table of Contents

# Chapter One
# An Introduction to Materials Development

## Introduction

There is a notorious shortage of teaching materials for the Less Commonly Taught Languages (LCTLs)—usually defined as any language except English, French, German, and Spanish. With a few notable exceptions, LCTL coursebooks tend to be outdated, dull, and oriented primarily towards grammar, while supplementary materials usually are unavailable. Most LCTL teachers I know create or adapt many of their own teaching materials; yet it is often difficult to know exactly what to do with the materials one has. This book aims to provide both principles and practical guidelines for turning "raw materials" into activities for the language classroom.

Of course, it is impossible to provide actual teaching materials for all the LCTLs in a source like this: Recall that there are about 6,000 languages in the world, several hundred of which are regularly taught in the U.S. alone. This book, however, will provide examples from a wide range of languages; in several cases we will use English, as the language we have in common. None of this will relieve you, the teacher, of the need to produce your own materials. However, we will provide both general principles and directions of thinking to suggest approaches to the use of materials, and also a wide range of specific suggestions for ways in which to use different kinds of materials.

In fact, I believe that it is right that teachers should prepare some of their own materials. Most teachers of ESL (English as a Second Language) do so, for instance, despite the large number of commercially published materials available. Why is this so? There are at least two important reasons. First, working on your own materials gives you a sense of control and ownership, whereas using other people's materials encourages dependence on them. Second, only you know your learners, what their interests are, and what they will find fun and engaging. Creating one's own materials, in my view, is an important part of being an independent, professional teacher. This is an important aspect of the philosophy underlying this book.

What do I mean by "materials"? Basically, "materials" can be anything that stimulates the use of language in a language classroom. Usually the materials themselves involve the target language (the language being taught): menus, poems, recipes, newspaper articles, etc. Often they also convey cultural information—movies or novels, for instance. An important principle is that materials do not necessarily have to provide a lot of language content themselves; a wide range of materials can be used primarily to stimulate language production and comprehension on the part of the students—or, to put it in more human terms, can get them involved in using the language for purposes of real communication.

In this book, when I say "raw materials" I mean materials which have been taken from a non-teaching context and which have not yet been prepared for teaching. This may be an article cut out of a newspaper or magazine, a photograph, a video of a TV show, a poem, or any number of other things. "Teaching materials" are what you prepare for the classroom using these raw materials. Thus, you may decide to use only part of a newspaper article; you give the students a scrambled version of part of the text, then a copy of the whole text, and you prepare a student worksheet that includes a pre-reading task, some discussion questions, some vocabulary work, and a follow-up writing assignment. All these are the teaching materials.

Language teaching professionals often emphasize the importance of using "authentic" materials—that is, materials taken from real-life contexts beyond the classroom, such as target-language newspapers, short stories, TV news, websites, and so on. How important is it to use only such authentic materials? A couple of points need to be made in this regard.

First, it's very important that language learners overcome as quickly as possible the anxiety induced by seeing and hearing the target language in use. In the language classroom we sometimes cosset our students, "protecting" them from texts that we deem too hard for them. But this is a mistake. An example from my own experience: I studied Russian for several years, but my encounters with the language were limited to our very traditional coursebooks and to nineteenth-century literature. I never felt comfortable looking through *Pravda* or watching a contemporary Russian movie, because such materials were never used in my class. I completely lacked early and extensive exposure to the language as it's used today. To avoid such a situation, it is good to get students used to seeing and interacting with authentic materials as soon as possible in the learning process.

Second, while we sometimes find ourselves writing texts for learners, it's always harder to write authentic-sounding language than to find it. Third, the "feel" of authentic materials is also an important element—it gives learners a sense of a direct encounter with the target language and culture that cannot otherwise be had. Fourth, second language users in the world outside the language classroom frequently come up against words, expressions, or references that they do not know or understand; becoming a competent speaker of the language does not mean knowing the language in its entirety, but learning how to deal with unknown language in a way that doesn't paralyze you. This can only happen by getting used to the complexities and colloquialisms of real language in use.

There is an important flip side to this, however, and one which I will be stressing throughout this book. In order to be able to interact with authentic texts, it is absolutely essential that learners have a clear, delineated task which can be carried out successfully without understanding every word of the text. If you're reading a restaurant menu, for example, you don't need to know every word of every dish to figure out how much things cost, or to find a dish that you would like. If you're studying a map, you don't have to know all the words that appear on it in order to find your way from one location to another. It is crucial, then, that the tasks we devise using authentic materials can be carried out with an imperfect knowledge of the language the materials contain. It is precisely this process—achieving something despite not understanding the entire text—that will give learners the confidence to be able to operate successfully in the target language (that is, the language they are learning).

## What We Know About Second Language Learning and Teaching

Julian Edge, a noted specialist in teacher development, has said that he is trying to eradicate the word "apply"—as in "applying theory"—from his professional vocabulary. He argues that what teachers should do is not to try to apply theory but to try to theorize practice—that is, to reflect on what works and what doesn't in their classrooms, and to draw out principles of language teaching from the understandings they gain from this reflection.

I happen to agree with Edge, and I will not suggest here that you "apply" particular theories of language learning in the materials you develop. Nevertheless, I've been in the field of language learning and teaching for many years now, and I'm increasingly struck by the simple consonance between what research has shown us about language learning and what kinds of materials work well in classes. For this reason, I summarize below some of the things we know about how people (especially adults) learn second or foreign languages, not because this will suggest radically different ways of doing things, but because it will offer support for certain practices that many experienced teachers already know to work well in language teaching. Many of us have found it useful to bear these facts in mind as we develop materials or evaluate existing materials.

- In both L1 (first or native language) and L2 (second or foreign language, the language being learned), reading, listening, and viewing are inherently active processes in which learners actively construct meaning and respond to what they read or see.

- Left to their own devices, successful readers (in both L1 and L2) are usually able to take in the meaning of a text without getting "hung up" on the form—remembering vocabulary, noticing grammar etc.

- Extensive vocabulary learning is essential if learners are to be able to express themselves effectively and appropriately in the second language.

- Existing education systems often encourage a passive and plodding approach to reading and listening. Learners feel that they have to understand every word (and that the teacher's job is to provide this understanding, usually through direct translation). This has been found to be an ineffective and often counterproductive way of learning a language.

- Encouraging good strategy use—e.g. being able to guess the meaning of words from context—is a vital part of teaching a language.

- Learners learn better through intrinsically interesting material with intrinsically interesting content.

- Learners are entirely capable of interacting with (and using) authentic target-language texts of various kinds, provided the tasks they are given are appropriate for them.

- Learners learn more when they are given a choice of texts, subject matter and so on: in other words, when they have a sense of control over their own learning.

## Principles of Materials Design

As above with the idea of "applying theory," the following principles of materials design are not theoretical rules to be followed blindly, but are simply guidelines that have emerged from the work of many experienced teachers in the area of materials design and development. Rather than acting as restrictions, they are intended to remind us of what possibilities exist when we first look at raw materials with a view to using them in the classroom. As the book progresses I'll say more about these principles; but for the moment let them serve as an introduction to the kinds of ideas and activities I'll be suggesting in the book.

1. Anything can be used as material.
2. Texts are not sacred—they can be altered or played with.
3. Topics should be specific, not general.
4. Look at content and meaning first, form (e.g. grammar and vocabulary) later.
5. Use materials as interactively as possible.

6. Focus on what will stimulate the students' interest, imagination, and creativity.

7. Wherever possible, integrate materials.

8. Vary the task, not just the text.

9. Keep things simple—this applies both to layout and instructions.

10. Keep an open mind about how texts can be used for different purposes.

## Developing Language Materials: Two Examples

At this point I'd like to show in practice what kinds of materials and activities can be produced when you try to follow the preceding principles and guidelines. In this section we'll look at two sets of materials, the first in English and the second in Polish, each developed around a reading text. The first one is very simple, and shows that materials development doesn't have to be done on a huge scale—it just needs to be interesting and engaging. The second example shows a much more extensive set of materials that illustrate the principles listed above.

### *Example One: Sears Tower Facts and Figures*

The first example is taken from a "Teach Yourself English" book written for publication in Poland (Johnston & Rydel-Johnston, 2001). The main character in the book, Anna, a young Polish teacher, visits Chicago for two weeks; the lessons and activities are built around that visit. In one chapter Anna visits the Sears Tower. The activity here is based on an authentic text: a free flyer in which facts and figures about the tower are given. I prepared a list of questions to which answers can be found in the flyer; but learners are asked to guess the answers to the questions *before* they look at it. In this way, I tried to create an active approach to the reading and to give readers a purpose for looking at the text—and one they could achieve without understanding every word. If I were using this text in class, I would probably begin with a more general discussion for a minute or two to ask what the students already know about the Sears Tower. Then I'd give them the questions and ask them to speculate in pairs or small groups about the answers. Only then would they get to see the reading and be asked to check their answers. I might even give candies to the pair or group whose guesses were the closest! The point is that the text is being used not primarily as a source of language input (such as learning new vocabulary), but as a stimulus for spoken language—though that spoken language will of course involve the new vocabulary contained in the text.

The text from the flyer appears on p. 5. The questions were as follows:

1. How high is the Sears Tower?

2. How much did it cost to build?

3. How many tourists come to the tower per year?

4. How many steps are there to the top?

5. How far can you see from the top?

6. How much does the building weigh?

7. How fast do the elevators move?

8. How much telephone cable is there in the building?

**Example One: The Sears Tower**

# SEARS TOWER

## FACTS AND FIGURES

- America's Tallest Building!
- 110 stories, 1,454 feet high.
- 1,707 feet including twin antenna towers.
- More than 43,000 miles of telephone cable.
- More than 2,000 miles of electrical wire.
- Opened in 1973, taking three years to build.
- The cost of building Sears Tower was in excess of $150 million.
- 4.5 million gross square feet of floor space.
- The Tower's framework consists of 76,000 tons of steel, has more than16,000 bronze-tinted windows, and has 28 acres of black duranodic aluminum skin.
- The building contains enough concrete to build an eight-lane highway five miles long.
- Sears Tower elevators operate as fast as 1,600 feet per minute.
- More than 1.5 million tourists visit the Skydeck each year.
- More than 25,000 miles of plumbing.
- More than 25,000 entries into the building daily.
- The combined weight of the building is 222,500 tons.
- On a clear day, visibility from the Skydeck is more than 40-50 miles.
- There are 2,232 steps from ground level to the roof.

**Sears Tower Skydeck**
233 South Wacker Drive
Chicago, Illinois 60606
312.875.9696

Opens at 9:00 a.m. seven days a week, 365 days a year.

Reservations can be arranged for group tours by calling:
312.875.9447

Several of the principles referred to above can be seen at work in this example. The topic is a very specific one (Principle 3); the focus is on content, not language (Principle 4); the materials are being used interactively (Principle 5); and the activity is kept simple in structure (Principle 9).

### Example Two: Like a Stone into Water

The second example revolves around a reading text for an intermediate Polish class. I developed these materials with two colleagues, Czesia Kolak and Ania Franczak, at a workshop run by the University of Hawaii's National Foreign Language Resource Center. Let's see step by step how we went from the "raw materials"—an article in a magazine—to the finished teaching materials, which are designed to cover several hours of class time.

The materials described here formed one half of a unit on crime; the other half was designed around a short video extract from a news broadcast recorded from SCOLA. The reading passage was taken from *Kobieta i Życie,* a general interest magazine aimed at women, rather like *Woman's Day* in the U.S. It is an article about people who disappear without a trace—"like a stone into water," a Polish expression that serves as the title of the article. The original article by Katarzyna Stawiska appears below.

---

**Example Two: Like a Stone Into Water**

## JAK KAMIEŃ W WODĘ

**Pierwsza część**

Anna Semczuk i Ernestyna Wieruszewska, uczennice warszawskiego LO im. Władysława IV, w piątek 22 stycznia wyjechały na dawno zaplanowane, wymarzone zimowe wakacje do Zakopanego. Zatrzymały się u zaprzyjaźnionej gaździny w Kościelisku. Zatelefonowały do rodziców, że dojechały szczęśliwie. Z zapisków Anki wiadomo, co dziewczyny robiły, gdzie były w sobotę, niedzielę, poniedziałek. We wtorek rano, 26 stycznia wyszły do miasta; ostatni raz widziano je na dworcu PKP, kupowały bilety powrotne do domu. A potem ślad po nich zaginął. . .

W połowie marca dwie poznańskie studentki: 21-letnia Iwona Gołębiowska i 20-letnia Hanna Waszkowiak wybrały się na weekend do stadniny w Sierakowie, w województwie gorzowskim. Hanna przepadała za jazdą konną, ilekroć mogła wyjeżdżać z miasta; zwykle zatrzymywała się u tego samego gospodarza, w pobliskiej wsi Zwierzyniec. W tamtą, krytyczną sobotę 13 marca, przyjechała z koleżanką i psem. Kiedy w poniedziałek nie pojawiła się w domu, rodzina zaalarmowała policję. Okazało się wówczas, że nie ma również wiadomości o Iwonie. Dziewczyny zniknęły, jak kamień w wodzie. Został tylko ulubiony pies Hanny.

W pierwszym wypadku przetrząśnięto Tatry, zrozpaczeni rodzice Anny i Ernestyny na własną rękę przeszukali bodaj każdy metr kwadratowy Zakopanego i okolic. Szukali swoich córek w całej Polsce. Odwołali się do pomocy jasnowidzów i wróżbitów, którzy utrzymywali, że dziewczęta żyją, ale są siłą przetrzymywane. . . Gdzie? Na to pytanie odpowiedzi nie ma.

W drugim przeczesano nadnoteckie lasy, akweny, wsie. Oczywiście przesłuchano gospodarza, u którego zatrzymały się Iwona i Hanna. Utrzymywał on, że w nocy z soboty na niedzielę doszło do kłótni między nim a dziewczynami. Ponoć opuściły one jego dom i udały się. . . no właśnie, dokąd? Zwierzyniec położony jest na odludziu, do najbliższego przystanku autobusowego kawałek drogi. Czy dziewczęta wyruszyły w nocną wędrówkę? A jeżeli tak, dlaczego zostawiły psa?

**Druga część**

Co roku do Wydziału Poszukiwań Osób Zaginionych KG Policji trafi jak mówi podkomisarz Renata Piątkowska, około 11 tysięcy zgłoszeń. Prawie jedna trzecia z nich (około 4 tysięcy) dotyczy zaginięć młodzieży w wieku od 14 do 17 lat. Ucieczki z domów, bo głównie są to ucieczki, niebezpiecznie nasilają się u progu lub podczas wakacji. Powody, jak to w życiu, bywają całkiem błahe i nader dramatyczne. Ucieka się więc z domu, bo na świadectwie dwójka, jedna, druga, za które ojciec niechybnie złoi skórę. Ucieka się, bo rodzice piją i biją, ale także dlatego, że nie umieją lub nie chcą kochać. Ucieka się nie tylko z domów, w których bieda aż piszczy, ale także z tych, gdzie wydawałoby się nie brakuje ptasiego mleka. Ucieka się z powodu zawodu miłosnego.

Częściej wyskakują z domu po zapałki i nie wracają mężczyźni. Kobietom na taki krok trudniej się zdecydować. Prawie 3 tysiące Polaków rocznie ucieka od dotychczasowego życia, i całkiem świadomie pragnie zerwać i z przeszłością, i z uwierającą teraźniejszością. Policja odnajduje ich i wtedy okazuje się, że większość z nich nie chce wracać tam, skąd odeszła, pragnie zatrzeć za sobą ślady.

Przyczyną blisko tysiąca zaginięć (te dane odnoszą się wprawdzie do ubiegłego roku, ale właściwie nie zmieniają się od lat) są choroby psychiczne, przede wszystkim, choć nie tylko, zaniki pamięci.

Dwieście, dwieście pięćdziesiąt osób ulega co roku nieszczęśliwym wypadkom, i to często trudnym do przewidzenia (np. jakaś kobieta wybrała się sama na grzyby, dostała zawału serca, zmarła w lesie, jej ciało odnaleziono po pewnym czasie, czy inny przykład: mężczyzna skracał drogę do domu przechodząc przez zamarzniętą rzekę, lód załamał się, zwłoki odnaleziono dopiero wiosną).

Ludzie czasem uciekają od świata, popełniają samobójstwo gdzieś na odludziu, w lesie, w górach, rzucają się pod pociąg w odległym od domu miejscu (takich nieszczęśliwych zdarzeń w ubiegłym roku naliczono 135). Natomiast 22 osoby padły ofiarą zabójstwa.

Ponad 90 procent osób zaginionych, których nazwiska trafiły do KG Policji, wcześniej czy później odnajduje się. Czasem trwa to lata, na przykład wtedy, gdy ktoś opuścił Polskę, wtedy często szuka się pomocy w Interpolu.

Ale aż tysiąc osób rocznie ginie bez śladu. I zapewne nigdy nie dowiemy się, czy i jak zgasła ich gwiazda. . .

**Level:**

Upper Intermediate

**Skill(s):**

Reading

# JAK KAMIEŃ W WODĘ

## ☞ PRZED CZYTANIEM

- Za chwilę przeczytasz tekst. Tytuł tego tekstu jest "Jak kamień w wodę". W parze z partnerem pomyśl co to znaczy i o czym może być ten tekst.

- Popatrz na ogłoszenie. W parze z partnerem odpowiedz na następujące pytania:

  1. Co się stało?

  2. Jakie informacje zawiera ogłoszenie?

  3. Kto zwykle wydaje takie ogłoszenia?

  4. Gdzie się je wywiesza?

# ZAGINIONA

Anna Semczuk, l. 17, zam. w Warszawie, córka Witolda i Marii Semczuków. 165 cm wzrostu, 52 kg, ciemne blond włosy.

Zaginęła w dn. 26.01.93 w Zakopanem; ostatni raz widziana na dworcu PKP.

Z wszelkimi informacjami prosimy dzwonić na tel.: 73-92-01

## ☐ CZYTANIE

• Przeczytaj pierwszą część tekstu, która opowiada dwie historie o tajemniczych zniknięciach. Dla każdej z tych historii odpowiedz na następujące pytania:

|  | Historia I | Historia II |
|---|---|---|
|  |  |  |
| Kto zginął? |  |  |
| Jaką akcję podjęto? |  |  |
| Kto podjął akcję? |  |  |
| Czy problem został rozwiązany? |  |  |

• Przyszedłeś na policję, żeby zgłosić zaginięcie Iwony Gołębiowskiej. Wypełnij policyjny druk.

**KOMISARIAT POLICJI W SIERAKOWIE**
**ul. Powstańców Śląskich 25**
**54-792 Sieraków**
**tel. 73-58**

### ZGŁOSZENIE ZAGINIĘCIA

Dane dotyczące zaginionego/zaginionej:

Nazwisko _____ Imię _____

Wiek _____ Płeć _____

Miejsce stałego pobytu _____

Zawód _____

Dane dotyczące zaginięcia:

Ostatnio widziana:

    Miejscowość _____ woj._____

    Data _____

    Godz. _____

    Przez kogo _____

Inne uwagi _____

_____

_____

_____

Osoba zgłaszająca zaginięcie_____

_____ , dn. _____ .

- Przeczytaj uważnie drugą część tekstu. Odpowiedz na pytania:

  1.  Ile osób ginie co roku?

  2.  Jaki procent z nich się odnajduje?

- Tekst wymienia siedem głównych powodów zaginięć. Korzystając z tekstu zidentyfikuj je i wpisz je pod odpowiednimi numerami:

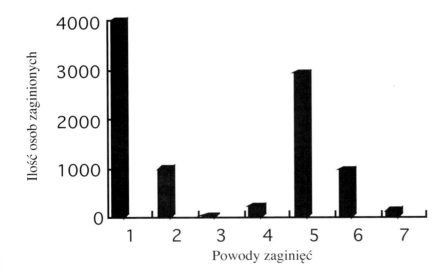

1. _____        5. _____

2. _____        6. _____

3. _____        7. _____

4. _____

## ☐ ĆWICZENIA JĘZYKOWE

• Przeczytaj czasowniki po lewej stronie i połącz je linią z odpowiednimi rzeczownikami po prawej stronie.

| | |
|---|---|
| zerwać | samobójstwo |
| ulegać | ślady |
| zatrzec | zabójstwa |
| odwołać się | z przeszłością |
| alarmować | do pomocy |
| padać ofiarą | kamień w wodzie |
| znikać jak | policję |
| popełnić | nieszczęśliwym wypadkom |

## ☐☐ ROZMOWA

• Jesteś ostatnią osobą, która widziała Iwonę Gołębiowską. Opowiedz, co robiła, jak była ubrana, jak się zachowywała, etc.

## ☐ PISANIE

• Opisz historię o tym jak zgubiłeś się w lesie, obcym mieście, etc.

## Stage 1: Point of Entry

To start, we needed a *point of entry* into the text: a task that would engage the learners' attention and make them interested in reading (there will more about points of entry in Chapter Two). We did this in two stages. First, we asked students to speculate briefly on the title and what it might mean, deliberately withholding for the moment the meaning of this expression ("like a stone into water"). Second, using an old photograph, we prepared a mock-up of a "MISSING" ("ZAGINIONA") poster which was given to the students before they received the reading passage. The information from the poster is taken from the reading and matches the kind of thing one finds on such posters. The task asks the students to discuss in Polish the following questions: What happened? What information appears in the poster? Who usually puts up such posters? Where are they put? The poster was designed to do several things at once: to provide a task that involved only a small amount of language and thus could be completed quickly; to get students curious about the upcoming text; and to give them some of the materials in the text ahead of time so that there would be "islands of security" in the text where they were sure they understood the meaning without too much effort.

## Stage 2: Deciding How to Present the Text

As we (the materials developers) familiarized ourselves with the text, we realized that it fell quite neatly into two parts. The first concerned the disappearance of two pairs of girls in unrelated incidents in different parts of Poland. The second part gave more general information about such disappearances, including statistics. We decided to break the reading of the text into two parts also, and we labeled them "Part One" and "Part Two."

## Stage 3: Devising Tasks

In each case, we wanted to come up with a task or tasks that could be completed by the students without understanding every word of the text, which would be appropriate for the nature of the text, and which would give the students a sense of achievement. Different tasks seemed right for each part.

For the first part, we designed a simple grid in which the students had to fill in four pieces of information about each story:

|  | First Story | Second Story |
|---|---|---|
| Who disappeared? |  |  |
| What action was taken? |  |  |
| Who took this action? |  |  |
| Was the problem solved? |  |  |

The idea of this task was to extract the most important information from the text—matching the purpose of a native speaker reader, for whom this information would be the most salient and interesting.

Second, we made another mock-up, this time of a police station form for reporting the disappearance of an individual. We chose another one of the people mentioned in the text, and created a form in which students have to fill in such details as name, age, gender, where and when she was last seen, and so on. Most though not all of this information is contained in the story; students are to fill in as many details as they can find in the text. With both these activities, our goal was to encourage an interactive approach to the reading of the passage, and to give the students something to do with the passage rather than just reading it passively.

We noticed that the second part of the reading contained statistics relating to the numbers of people who disappear, the percentage of them who are found, and seven different causes of disappearances (people who simply want to disappear, people killed in accidents, suicides, and so on). Our task had two parts. First, students had to find answers to two basic questions: How many people disappear each year; and what percentage of them is found? Second, we created a chart to show the relative numbers of those who fall into each category of disappearance. The columns of various sizes were numbered; the students' job was to find the seven causes and match them up with the right column. Once again, the goal was to provide a manageable task which could be completed without understanding everything in the text, but which required the students to focus on the most important (and interesting) information it contains.

## Stage 4: Identifying Language to Work On

Lastly, we added a short language exercise: an activity drawing conscious and explicit attention to aspects of language such as grammar and vocabulary. (Our goal in the workshop was primarily to produce communicative materials in the areas of reading and listening, and so we paid less attention to work on language, though more could definitely be done here.) Since the learners were intermediate level, we felt that collocations were particularly important for them. We chose eight verb + complement combinations (e.g. to commit + suicide, to notify + the police), mixed them up in two columns, and asked learners to match them up without looking at the text. This is a kind of exercise that requires recognition rather than recall, and is good for language that the learners might not be able to use actively but should be able to comprehend when they read or hear it. (Some of this language was recycled in the video part of the unit.)

It will be repeated here often that it is a good idea to leave language work until after you have looked at content; students can't do both at once, and they need to be weaned off the conviction that they have to understand every single word before they can even begin to read the text.

## Stage 5: Devising Follow-up Activities

As with the language exercises, our focus was on communicative use of the materials themselves, so we did not develop follow-up activities as much as we could have. We suggest a speaking activity in which the last person to see one of the missing women describes what she looked like, how she was dressed, how she was behaving and so on; then a writing task in which the student describes a time he or she got lost in the woods, an unfamiliar city, or somewhere else.

## Summary

These examples have served several purposes. We have seen some of the kinds of activities that can be developed on the basis of authentic materials. Second, I have tried to make explicit the thought processes that teachers go through as they figure out what can be done with the raw materials they have chosen. Lastly, it can be seen how these kinds of activities follow the guidelines given above.

In this case, the "Missing" text accords amongst others with Principle 2 (texts are not sacred—they can be cut up, adapted, presented in parts, and so on); Principle 3 (once again this topic is a very specific one); Principle 4 (focus on content before focusing on form, i.e. doing language work only later); Principle 5 (note how interactive the activities are); and Principle 6 (focus on what the students find interesting).

## Gathering Materials: Some Hints

The first principle mentioned above is that anything can be used as material for language teaching. This includes both materials that involve use of the language in question—written or spoken texts—and non-verbal materials such as pictures. A Polish teacher of English, Bartek Madejski, once took a recording of a very beautiful Vietnamese folk song to class; he played it to his (also Polish) students and asked them to "translate" the words of the song (which of course no-one understood) into English. The results were wonderful, creative "translations" based on the students' emotional and aesthetic responses to the song. This is what is meant by saying that anything can be used as material in language classes.

Collect as wide a range of raw materials as you can from the culture in which your language is spoken, and think as broadly as possible about what to collect. Often, objects that seem not to offer much in the way of language input are interesting in themselves and generate discussion and reflection—a streetcar ticket, for instance, a stamp, or an advertisement from a magazine. In general, while pieces of extensive text, such as magazine articles, may be good for higher-level learners, for others it is often better to look for objects with relatively little writing and/or extensive visuals (we'll see examples of this kind of thing in subsequent chapters).

The following is a partial list of the kinds of things that can be used in developing teaching materials for class:

| Written Materials: | | Video or DVD: | CD or Cassette |
|---|---|---|---|
| recipes | personality tests | feature films | pop songs |
| health brochures | menus | documentaries | interviews |
| maps | receipts | news programs | folk songs |
| theater programs | quizzes | silent films | books or poetry on tape |
| movie reviews | cartoons | situation comedies | comedy recordings |
| instructions | TV guides | talk shows | |
| packaging | horoscopes | television commercials | |
| newspaper headlines | tourist literature | music videos | |
| magazine advertisements | | | |
| timetables for buses, trains, excursions | | | |

## Overview of the Book

The five chapters that follow offer suggestions and examples for the development of language teaching materials in various formats. Chapter Two looks at reading materials, focusing first on the exploitation of various "authentic materials"—newspaper articles, brochures, maps, menus and the like—and then on the use of literature. Chapter Three looks at listening materials, including songs and recorded materials, and also making your own recorded materials. Chapter Four concentrates on using video and other moving images, while Chapter Five offers ways of making use of pictures, photographs, cartoons and so on. Finally, Chapter Six argues for the importance of an integrated skills (i.e. topic-based) approach, and shows some examples of integrated skills packets. In Appendix I you will find a number of web-based resources for materials development, while Appendix II provides information about copyright in the context of language teaching.

As a supplement to this printed book, the LCTL project at CARLA maintains a related Internet site. On these pages you can find updates, more examples, and a forum for discussing the ideas and practices presented in this book. The site's location is: http://carla.umn.edu/lctl/development.

Each chapter will take roughly the same format. We'll begin with a few words about what is known about second language learning and use in relation to the kinds of material in question. We then suggest a set of guidelines or principles to keep in mind while developing materials. After that, the bulk of each chapter is devoted to a series of suggestions for activities and uses of texts, illustrated with a broad range of examples from various languages. Each chapter then closes with a set of resources, including recommendations of particularly useful books and articles.

As mentioned at the beginning of this introductory chapter, it's obviously impossible to provide materials for every one of the less commonly taught languages. The aim of this book is to offer ideas for ways in which materials in various languages can be exploited; it is with that goal in mind that comments are provided on the sample activities reproduced here. It is not possible to offer extensive materials for the language or languages you teach; what we hope to do is to give you a variety of ways of thinking about how to use different kinds of materials. If at least some of these ideas inspire you enough to try them out, the book will have been successful.

## Resources

If you're interested in reading more about second language learning, a good place to start is:

Lightbown, P. M., & Spada, N. (2006). *How languages are learned* (3rd ed.). Oxford: Oxford University Press.

There are very few books and articles written specifically about how to create materials and how to use them in the classroom. The following sources may be of some help. In each chapter, we will also list some of the better books containing suggestions of how to use specific kinds of materials— literature, reading texts, listening materials, computer-based materials and so on.

Byrd, P. (Ed.). (1994). *Material writer's guide*. New York: Heinle & Heinle.

Larimer, R. E., & Schleicher, L. (Eds.). (1999). *New ways in using authentic materials in the classroom*. Alexandria, VA: TESOL.

Tomlinson, B. (Ed.). (1998). *Materials development in language teaching*. Cambridge: Cambridge University Press.

I also recommend two series that offer lots of practical, creative ideas for using authentic materials in the language classroom:

*New Ways Series*, published by TESOL; see the full list of titles on their website at: http://www.tesol. org.

*Resource Books for Teachers* (series editor Alan Maley), published by Oxford University Press, and also their *Resource Books for Teachers of Young Students*; see the full list of titles at: http://www.us.oup. com/us/corporate/publishingprograms/esl/titles/booksforteachers/?view=usa.

# Chapter Two
# Using Written Texts: Reading and Beyond

## Introduction

In this chapter we'll explore ways of making use of various kinds of written text. The chapter comprises two main sections. The first looks at how to use a variety of written "authentic materials" (see previous chapter) such as brochures, newspaper and magazine articles, recipes, menus and the like. The second considers ways of using literature—poems, short stories, extracts from plays and novels—in the language classroom.

The chapter begins with an outline of what we know about how second language learners read texts, and then sets out some broad principles that guide the creation of the kinds of activities and uses of materials shown in the chapter.

## How Second Language Learners Read

The first thing that needs to be said about reading in a second language is that the underlying psychological processes are in fact little different from reading in one's native language. Of course, second language readers, much more frequently than first language readers, encounter problems with unknown words, phrases, grammar, and cultural contextual information; and to some extent different strategies may be employed when reading a radically different kind of writing system, for example when American students used to the alphabetic script of English have to read a logographic, or word-based, script like that used for Chinese. Nevertheless, it is a mistake to think that this makes the reading process different in some fundamental way.

Quite another matter, however, is the fact that some people are better readers than others. Interestingly, research has shown that those people who read well (effectively, efficiently, with pleasure) in their first language usually transfer these skills to reading in the second language, while those who have problems reading in the first language also have problems in the second language. It is also true that many second language learners are taught approaches to reading that emphasize, for example, the need to understand every word of a text, or suggest that "understanding" a text means being able to translate it. These habits form an additional barrier to effective and enjoyable reading in the second language.

What is said in this chapter, then, in fact applies both to first and second language reading, though its significance in terms of language teaching is something that we language teachers must figure out for ourselves.

### Reading as an Active Process

To begin with, one crucial point needs to be made: All reading is *active*. Most of us think of reading as a passive process whereby printed information is transferred from the page via our eyes to our brain. This is certainly part of what is going on; but such a picture ignores the central fact that at the same time as our eyes are receptively taking in the text, our brain is working actively to make sense of the information, and it often does so in a way that adds something to the text or changes it in some way. Take this very simple example. Turn the page and immediately read aloud the text in the box at the top:

## A NIGHT
## AT THE
## THE OPERA

It often takes people a good few seconds to notice that the text actually includes the word "the" twice. If reading really did involve simply looking at the text, we would not make this mistake. So why do we in fact fail to see the "full" text? The reason is simple yet crucial to the reading process: When we read, as information comes in from the page our brain begins to work actively to make sense of it, and it can only do so in an efficient way by taking shortcuts such as predicting what's going to come next. By the time we reach "A Night At The...", our knowledge of the world is such that the next word could well be "Opera"—that's what we expect. Since our eyes immediately register just that word in the text, we skip over the second "The" because we're not expecting it.

All reading involves this active process. We don't always make this kind of mistake, but only because most texts are in fact fairly predictable, and don't try to trip us up like the text above did. Nevertheless, our brain is always one step ahead of the text, actively anticipating what will come next.

One other important way in which the brain works actively is to fill in the missing details in a text. No text contains every piece of information relating to its subject. There's always something that the reader needs to add. For instance, look at the following short poem by William Carlos Williams:

**The Loving Dexterity**

The flower
    fallen
she saw it

    where
it lay
    a pink petal

intact
    deftly
placed it

    on
its stem
    again

Now, consider these two questions about the text:

1. What does the flower look like?
2. What does the hand look like?

When a reader pictures the scene described in the poem, she or he has to add this information, since the poet doesn't tell us what kind of flower it is (other than that it is a pink one), nor does he describe the hand, yet we have to picture both in imagining the scene. Thus, reading is active: The reader brings information and understanding to the text as well as taking information from it. If you were going to use this poem in a language class, the two questions posed above would make a good opening activity after the learners had read or listened to the poem a couple of times.

## Three Dimensions of the Reading Experience

In general, three aspects of the reading process will guide the suggestions made in this chapter. They are: *meaning; purpose;* and *response.* Each of these is discussed in more detail below.

### *Meaning*

The study of how second language learners approach reading has shown convincingly that when language learners read a text, if left to their own devices (without a teacher to direct them otherwise), they focus first on the meaning of the text, not its form. In other words, they try to extract information from the text concerning its content, and do not initially pay special attention to grammar or vocabulary. This is in striking contrast to what teachers often do with written texts in classrooms—beginning with a detailed study of the vocabulary and grammar of the text, and only later moving on to what it is about—that is, reading it as a text.

Language should be *about* something other than itself—we should learn Chinese, or Polish, or Urdu in order to be able to find out about the world from texts written in those languages. Thus, all the activities suggested in this book start from the meaning of a text, and only when some work with the meaning has been done do students begin to look at the language. (We saw this in Chapter One with the text on disappearances.) Experience shows that this approach leads to more engagement in learning and to livelier, more successful lessons.

Several important consequences follow from the approach outlined here. First, while some preparatory work on language is sometimes necessary, pre-teaching of vocabulary should be absolutely *kept to a minimum*—only those words or phrases that are completely essential in dealing with the text should be pre-taught. Rather than exhaustive preparations for reading, what we need to look for is a *point of entry* into the text—a way of engaging the learner's interest.

Though learners should not be spoon-fed new vocabulary, they can be encouraged to actively anticipate the words and phrases they are likely to encounter in a text they are to read. This is often done in the form of a whole-class brainstorming activity. Preparing students in such a way is said to "activate their schema": in other words, it establishes or reinforces the associations between related words that, according to schema theory (see Resources below), makes reading easier and faster. Examples of this kind of preparatory activity will be seen in several of the examples in this chapter and elsewhere in the book.

Second, and closely connected, even apparently difficult texts can be used with low-level learners so long as the tasks assigned can be achieved by those learners. As Nunan puts it, "Vary the task, not the text" (1989, p. 51). An important related fact is that beginning learners need as early as possible to get over their fear of dealing with authentic texts, and to learn that they too can get something out of many kinds of text. This is a crucial part of our job as teachers. (For a good example of this principle in action, take a look at the first text in the examples given below—the Polish "Fala-Tour" advertisement.)

Third, it is important to recognize that meaning is not fully and unambiguously fixed in every text. Quite the opposite: Many texts are ambiguous and open-ended, and meaning is not fixed but negotiable. The poem by William Carlos Williams cited above is an example. Not only is uncertainty of meaning inevitable, it is actually an advantage in the classroom: Negotiation of meaning in conversation has been found to be an effective way of learning and using language, and the same surely applies to written texts. Thus, many of the activities described here involve the learners discussing potential meanings and interpretations of texts in class, as a fundamental part of the process of reading for meaning.

To sum up:

- The most interesting thing about a text is what it means, not the vocabulary or grammar it contains; second language readers instinctively know this and focus initially on meaning rather than on form.

- Given appropriate tasks, low-level learners can do useful work even with difficult texts.

- Meaning is rarely fixed; the process of finding meaning in the text is always simultaneously a process of interpretation. This process can be incorporated into the classroom.

## *Purpose*

Not all reading is the same. We read different texts in different ways. You probably need to pay much more careful attention to a recipe you are trying to follow than to a newspaper article about a foreign country. Likewise, you will read the report about the foreign country very differently if you happen to be about to travel to that country than if you are merely flipping through the paper over breakfast. Put briefly, the way that we read depends very much on our *purpose* in reading. Are we merely trying to extract information? Are we trying to bake a cake? catch a train? operate a VCR? fill in a passport application? *How* we read depends on *why* we read.

This fact has certain important consequences for the way we approach using written texts in the language classroom. First, it is very useful to ask ourselves: What purpose does a native speaker have in reading this text? While this shouldn't be the only way of thinking about activities around the text, it's a good place to start. Can we structure activities to recreate in some way that purpose? Second, it's important to *have* a purpose in addressing a text: Any activity should have some clearly defined goal that can be achieved by the learners. While the preceding consequences are widely agreed upon by many in the field, the position further taken here is that "reading in order to learn the language" is NOT an adequate purpose—language is not about itself, and texts are always about something else—whether it's soccer, knitting, medieval castles, dinosaurs, or whatever. And whatever the text is about, that's what our lessons should be about, and the activities we create should reflect this. (This approach was seen in the activities about the Sears Tower and "Like a Stone Into Water" that we looked at in Chapter One.)

Finally, it's important to remember that different people may have different purposes for reading the same text (indeed, the same person may have different purposes at different times). One American student may read about historical Kraków because she is studying for a PhD in history; another student may read the same text while thinking about her Polish ancestors; a third may be an avid traveler and be looking for interesting places to visit on an upcoming trip. There is nothing wrong with having such disparate purposes in the classroom; indeed, it is this that makes language teaching and learning so profoundly rich.

In brief:

- How we read depends crucially on why we read.

- Reading "to learn the language" is not an adequate purpose.

- The purposes of different individuals may be different even with the same text.

### Response

Recall the poem by William Carlos Williams cited above. You were asked to say what the flower was like and what the hand looked like, and we saw that since this information is not in the poem itself, it has to be supplied by the reader.

There is a further aspect to this, though, that is crucial in reading. Not only does this information have to be provided by the reader: *For each reader, the information is different.* One reader might imagine a rose; another a carnation; another an orchid. For one the hand might be that of a small child; for another it may belong to an old woman. Importantly, none of these responses is "correct" or "incorrect," since the poet doesn't specify; they are all possible, and they are all different. In other words, our response to reading is not only creative (that is, active), it is also individual and unique. This response is one of the most interesting and valuable aspects of the reading process, and is a wonderful source of ideas for activities around written texts in the classroom. To sum up:

- The most interesting thing about the reading process is the reader's response to the text.

- Each person's response is creative.

- Each person's response is different.

The sample materials shown below include examples of activities based on exploiting the differences amongst learners' responses to texts.

## Guidelines for the Development of Reading Materials

The preceding view of second language reading provides strong support for certain practical approaches to the use of written texts in language teaching. Many of these approaches are in fact already common practice in language teaching in many contexts; some resources are listed at the end of this chapter. The following points seem particularly salient (and will crop up as we look at suggestions and examples in the rest of the chapter):

- **Use all kinds of materials:** A very wide range of texts can be used for classroom use, from ticket stubs and cereal packets, through recipes and instructions, to informational leaflets, newspaper articles, horoscopes, personality quizzes—the list is endless, and is restricted only by what materials you can get your hands on and can find ways to use in class.

- **Look for a point of entry into the text:** The moment at which readers first engage with a text is an important one, and usually decides whether they will benefit from it and enjoy it or not. It's important to find an opening activity that will capture their interest and stimulate an active approach to reading. This kind of opening activity is referred to here as **a point of** entry into the text; it's also referred to as a pre-reading activity, though this term seems less dynamic.

- **Minimal pre-teaching of vocabulary:** It's important to wean students off the perceived need to understand every word of a text. This begins with pre-teaching: Give them only those words and phrases they absolutely need to begin to engage with the text.

- **Build activities around a purpose:** This may be the same purpose as a native speaker would have, or something different; but it's crucial that there be some goal involved towards which the activities lead.

- **Think about tasks:** Asking students to complete specific, attainable tasks gives them a sense of achievement; it also helps in reading with a purpose, and allows us to work with texts without understanding every word.

- **Texts are not sacred:** You can play with them, cut them up, change them for your own ends.

- **The learners are more important than the text!:** Focus on their interpretations and their responses, even where these may seem idiosyncratic.

- **Reading can be a social process:** Exploit the fact that a group of people is gathered in the classroom, and use the text as a springboard for a discussion of meanings, interpretations, and responses.

- **Integrate reading with the other skills:** As in the previous point, reading can be a starting-point for speaking, listening, and writing. This supports the goal of making reading active.

## *Using Written Texts: Examples*

In this section, you will see several examples of "everyday" texts being used for language teaching purposes; in each case, an attempt has been made to follow the principles outlined above. With each text salient features will be pointed out.

## Example 1: Fala-Tour (Polish, beginning level)

The first text is another Polish one. Imagine that you do not know any Polish at all (I expect that for the majority of my readers this is in fact true). Take a look at the Polish ad on the following page and try to answer the following questions:

1. What kind of company is advertised here?

2. What is the address and phone number of the company?

3. Find the Polish names for:

| | | |
|---|---|---|
| Australia | Israel | Portugal |
| Croatia | London | Spain |
| Egypt | Morocco | Switzerland |
| France | Paris | |

4. What do you think Włochy means? What about the word Góry?

5. What do you notice about how dates are written in Polish?

---

**Written Texts—Example 1: Fala-Tour**

CZŁONEK
POLSKIEJ
IZBY
TURYSTYKI

„Fala-Tour"
30-157 Kraków, ul. Kamienna 17
tel./fax (012) 2173349, 2178964, 7349216
www.falatour.pl        falatour@falatour.pl

## ZAPRASZA NA TANIE I ATRAKCYJNE IMPREZY

Paryż—
LOURDES,
LA SALETTE,
Zamki nad Loarą,
Szwajcaria,
Mont Blanc
29.06-05.07
06.08-15.08

Przewozy—
cała Europa,
tanie bilety
lotnicze,
wycieczki,
wczasy,
pielgrzymki,
ubezpieczenie,
wnajem
autokarów.

proponujemy sprzedaż korespondencyjną—zadzwoń lub mailuj

IZRAEL—EGIPT
zwiedzanie całej Ziemi Świętej i płn Egiptu.
Terminy:
25.04-09.05, 16-28.08, 07-19.09.

FATIMA—PORTUGALIA
ze zwiedzaniem całej Hiszpanii
Terminy:
02-20.05, 02-20.07, 02-20.08

MAROKO—
SAHARA—GÓRY ATLAS
Hiszpania—Francja—Włochy
Terminy:
14.06-02.07, 07.08-26.08, 09.09-28.09

Przyjmujemy
zamówienia
na wycieczki grupowe

AUSTRALIA
terminy
do uzgodnienia
(od 2 osób)

WŁOCHY—
Rzym, Capri
21.09-30.09
24.07-02.08

FRANCJA,
PORTUGALIA,
HISZPANIA,
IZRAEL,
CHORWACJA—
wycieczki, wczasy

LONDYN
27.05-03.06

Dogodne raty!

ZAPRASZAMY DO WSPÓŁPRACY PARAFIE, STOWARZYSZENIA, BIURA PODRÓŻY I SZKOŁY!

Dla grup zorganizowanych i dla rodzin preferencyjne zniżki.

*Answers to Fala-Tour:*

1.  The company is a travel agency.

2.  The company is located in Kraków (the city), at number 17, ul. Kamienna (Kamienna Street). Their three phone numbers appear below the address in the top right corner.

3.  The names of countries are as follows:

| | | |
|---|---|---|
| *Australia:* Australia | *Israel:* Izrael | Portugal: Portugalia |
| *Croatia:* Chorwacja | *London:* Londyn | Spain: Hiszpania |
| *Egypt:* Egipt | Morocco: Marok | Switzerland: Szwajcaria |
| *France:* Francja | Paris: Paryż | |

4.  Włochy means Italy (it contains Capri and also Rzym—Rome). Góry means mountains (Góry Atlas = Atlas Mountains).

5.  Polish dates are written with the day first, then the month (02.08 = August 2nd).

With absolutely no knowledge of Polish, it's still possible to complete a meaningful task such as this one and to learn some language in the bargain. If you had been asked to translate part of the text, or to answer comprehension questions related to the written text in the bottom left hand box, for instance, you wouldn't have been able to perform the task; but the tasks given above are manageable for complete beginners. This is what Nunan meant by saying: Vary the task, not just the text.

## Example 2: The L Game (English, lower intermediate)

The L Game was invented by Edward de Bono, a pioneer of lateral thinking in the 1970s and beyond. The game is very simple, and consists of manipulating L-shaped pieces and dots on a small board of 16 squares.

Students are divided into pairs and given the text "How to Play the L Game," along with a board and a set of playing pieces (these can be copied and cut up ahead of time). Their task is very simple—to play the game. To do this they have to read the fairly simple rules closely and accurately.

This activity is a good example of purpose—the learners have a clear and definable goal, and one moreover that goes beyond language into the real world. And little preparation is required!

The text, materials and detailed instructions are available online at: http://www.edwdebono.com/debono/lgame.htm.

## Example 3: Making Gado-gado (Indonesian, lower intermediate)

This example using a recipe for an Indonesian dish was cooked up (sorry, I couldn't resist) by Palsapah Aeni, Herlina Surbakti, and Christine Susanto of Jakarta International School. Like the previous one, it too revolves around a real-world purpose—that of following a recipe for making gado-gado, the national dish of Indonesia. Also like the previous example, it requires a close and accurate reading. The activities are carefully structured to lead from simple (naming ingredients) to more complex (rearranging cut-up text). Lots of cultural information is also provided. Special thanks to Margaretha Sudarsih of the University of Michigan for providing the recipe, the picture of the final meal, and the cloze exercise.

## Written Texts—Example 3: Making Gado-gado

**Unit:** Food

**Level:** Intermediate

**Grade:** Five

**Skill(s):** Reading

**Background Information:**

The students have already studied Indonesian measurements prior to this lesson.

**Summary of the Unit:**

· This unit is taught at the intermediate level of Grade 5. In this unit, students are studying about Indonesian food, restaurants, menus, and some recipes.

· In this sub-unit, the students will be studying the Gado-gado recipe. They will be able to understand what the ingredients are and know how to make it through the reading activity. They will also be able to cook it.

**Materials:**

· Pictures

· Handout/Worksheet

· Text of recipe for Gado-gado

**Pre-listening:**

Discussion about Indonesian food as well as Indonesian food with vegetable ingredients.

**Viewing:**

**Gado-gado**

*Photo courtesy of Margaretha Sudarsih*

1. **Elicit the Ingredients**

    T: Gambar apa ini? *(What is this a picture of?)*

    S: Gado-gado.

    T: Apa bahan-bahannya? *(What are the ingredients?)*

    S: _____

2. **Matching Activity**

Jodohkan gambar bahan-bahan untuk membuat "Gado-gado" dengan namanya. *(Match the pictures of Gado-gado ingredients with their names.)*

*Photos courtesy of Louis Janus*

II.

| | | |
|---|---|---|
| _____ timun | _____ jeruk nipis | _____ kacang tanah |
| _____ kentang | _____ kembang kol | _____ wortel |
| _____ kacang panjang | _____ kubis | _____ telur ayam |
| _____ cabai merah | _____ tauge | |

**Language Exercises:**

1. Jumbled sentences

   Bacalah kalimat-kalimat di bawah ini. Dengarkanlah kembali bagaimana membuat Gado-gado dan tulislah nomer di kolom yang kosong kalimat-kalimat tersebut sesuai dengan urutannya. *(Read the following sentences carefully. While listening, put them in order by numbering them.)*

   _____Kupas wortel, kukus sampai setengah matang saja, lalu potong-potong.

   _____Atur sayuran yang sudah direbus dan telor rebus serta tahu dan tempe goreng di satu piring. Tambahkan potongan mentimun dan tomat.

   _____Kukus buncis dan kol selama 5 menit saja, lalu angkat.

   _____Goreng kerupuk udang dengan sisa minyak goreng. Masukkan satu genggam kerupuk dalam sekali menggoreng. Jangan terlalu banyak.

   _____Waktu menghidangkan, setiap orang mengambil sayur rebus, tahu dan tempe goreng. Taruh potongan telor di atasnya. Siram dengan sambal kacang. Hiasi dengan potongan mentimun dan tomat. Tambahkan kerupuk.

   _____Rebus kentang sampai matang, tiriskan sampai dingin, kupas, lalu potong-potong (satu kentang dipotong menjadi 8 atau 10).

   _____Untuk sambalnya: goreng kacang tanah sampai matang. Atau, kalau tidak mau memakai minyak, bisa juga disangrai sampai matang.

   _____Tambahkan santan dan daun jeruk, lalu rebus dengan api kecil sambil diaduk. Usahakan supaya tidak terlalu encer dan tidak terlalu kental. Sesudah mendidih, angkat dan tuangkan ke dalam mangkok untuk disajikan.

   _____Masukkan kacang dalam blender, tambahkan bumbu yang sudah digerus dan sedikit air. lalu haluskan

   _____Rebus telor sampai matang, kupas, lalu iris masing-masing menjadi 4 bagian memanjang.

   _____Cuci kol dan iris tipis-tipis (seperti mi).

   _____Potong tahu dan tempe sebesar satu ruas jari. Goreng dengan minyak goreng: jangan bersama-sama, karena tahu makan waktu lebih lama. Goreng masin-masing sampai setengah matang saja.

   _____Keluarkan bumbu kacang dari blender dan masukkan ke dalam panci kecil.

   _____Sesudah buncis dicuci, masing-masing potong menjadi tiga bagian

   _____Gerus cabe, bawang putih, kencur, gula jawa dan garam.

2. Cloze exercise

   Isilah titik-titik dibawah ini dengan kata-kata yang tepat. *(Fill in the blanks with suitable words.)*

   _____ kentang sampai matang, _____ sampai dingin, _____, lalu _____ (satu kentang _____ menjadi 8 atau 10). _____ telor sampai matang, _____, lalu _____ masing-masing menjadi 4 bagian memanjang. _____ wortel, _____ sampai setengah matang saja, lalu _____. Sesudah buncis _____, masing-masing _____ menjadi tiga bagian. _____ kol dan _____ tipis-tipis (seperti mi). _____ buncis dan kol selama 5 menit saja, lalu _____.

   _____ tahu dan tempe sebesar satu ruas jari. _____ dengan minyak goreng: jangan bersama-sama, karena tahu makan waktu lebih lama. _____ masing-masing sampai setengah matang saja. _____ kerupuk udang dengan sisa minyak goreng. _____ satu genggam kerupuk dalam sekali menggoreng. Jangan terlalu banyak. Untuk sambalnya: _____ kacang tanah sampai matang. Atau, kalau tidak mau memakai minyak, bisa juga _____ sampai matang.

   _____ cabe, bawang putih, kencur, gula jawa dan garam. _____ kacang dalam blender, _____ bumbu yang sudah digerus dan sedikit air. Lalu _____. _____ bumbu kacang dari blender dan \_\_\_\_

____ ke dalam panci kecil. _____ santan dan daun jeruk, lalu _____ dengan api kecil sambil _____. Usahakan supaya tidak terlalu encer dan tidak terlalu kental. Sesudah mendidih, _____ dan _____ ke dalam mangkok untuk _____.

_____ sayuran yang sudah direbus dan telor rebus serta tahu dan tempe goreng di satu piring. _____ potongan mentimun dan tomat. Waktu menghidangkan, setiap orang mengambil sayur rebus, tahu dan tempe goreng. _____ potongan telor di atasnya. _____ dengan sambal kacang. _____ dengan potongan mentimun dan tomat. _____ kerupuk.

### Resep Gado-gado
*Untuk lima orang*

<u>Bahannya</u>

1 pon buncis

1 pon wortel

1 biji kol yang kecil

5 buah kentang sedang

1 pon tahu

1 pon tempe

30 gram minyak goreng

5 butir telor ayam

1 buah mentimun sedang, dipotong-potong

<u>Sambal Kacang</u>

200 gram kacang tanah

5 cabe rawit

4 siung bawang putih

10 gram gula jawa

1 ruas jari kencur atau 1 sendok teh kencur bubuk

2 lembar daun jeruk purut

1/2 kaleng santan

Garam secukupnya

<u>Cara membuatnya</u>:

1. Rebus kentang sampai matang, tiriskan sampai dingin, kupas, lalu potong-potong (satu kentang dipotong menjadi 8 atau 10).

2. Rebus telor sampai matang, kupas, lalu iris masing-masing menjadi 4 bagian memanjang.

3. Kupas wortel, kukus sampai setengah matang saja, lalu potong-potong.

4. Sesudah buncis dicuci, masing-masing potong menjadi tiga bagian.

5. Cuci kol dan iris tipis-tipis (seperti mi).

6. Kukus buncis dan kol selama 5 menit saja, lalu angkat.

7. Potong tahu dan tempe sebesar satu ruas jari. Goreng dengan minyak goreng: jangan bersama-sama, karena tahu makan waktu lebih lama. Goreng masin-masing sampai setengah matang saja.

8. Goreng kerupuk udang dengan sisa minyak goreng. Masukkan satu genggam kerupuk dalam sekali menggoreng. Jangan terlalu banyak.

9. Untuk sambalnya: goreng kacang tanah sampai matang. Atau, kalau tidak mau memakai minyak, bisa juga disangrai sampai matang.

10. Gerus cabe, bawang putih, kencur, gula jawa dan garam.

11. Masukkan kacang dalam blender, tambahkan bumbu yang sudah digerus dan sedikit air. lalu haluskan

12. Keluarkan bumbu kacang dari blender dan masukkan ke dalam panci kecil.

13. Tambahkan santan dan daun jeruk, lalu rebus dengan api kecil sambil diaduk. Usahakan supaya tidak terlalu encer dan tidak terlalu kental. Sesudah mendidih, angkat dan tuangkan ke dalam mangkok untuk disajikan.

14. Atur sayuran yang sudah direbus dan telor rebus serta tahu dan tempe goreng di satu piring. Tambahkan potongan mentimun dan tomat.

15. Waktu menghidangkan, setiap orang mengambil sayur rebus, tahu dan tempe goreng. Taruh potongan telor di atasnya. Siram dengan sambal kacang. Hiasi dengan potongan mentimun dan tomat. Tambahkan kerupuk.

Example 4: How to Perform Yoga (Korean, intermediate)

This set of materials is the work of Ji-Eun Kim of Brookhaven College. Yoga is of interest both to Americans and Koreans, and Ji-Eun Kim takes advantage of this fact, asking that students first discuss what they already know about yoga—a good example of how to make materials active. She then uses pictures to further draw on the students' own linguistic resources, before gradually moving towards a reading on the topic. She also provides an additional article for further reading. In these materials, note the nice balance between student contributions and provided text, and also the judicious and effective use of illustrations to support language learning.

### Written Text—Example 4: How to Perform Yoga

**Goals of the Lesson:**

- Students will learn vocabulary and expressions related to yoga exercises.
- Students will learn how to describe the various poses, positions, and/or motions: first as a verbal activity, then as a written one.
- Students will learn how to join two Korean clauses using Korean connectors.
- Students will learn how to omit the subject of a sentence.
- Based on the topic-based instructions, students will practice all four skills: speaking, listening, reading and writing.
- Students will become more familiar with authentic Korean texts.

**Material:**

Newspaper article "Yoga for Wellbeing" *NewsKorea,* July 17, 2004

**Level:** Intermediate and above

**Pre-reading Activities**

A. Discuss yoga with peers: e.g., Have you heard of yoga? If so, what do you know about it? What are some of the benefits of yoga? Have you taken a yoga lesson or class? Do you have any plans to learn yoga in the future? Does it look difficult to learn? What are some of your concerns about yoga (e.g., will you be able to master the positions? etc.).

B. Examine the following pictures: Observe the positions and describe them in Korean; guess the benefits of these poses.

C. Focus on key words: Write a short description of the positions based on the pictures and the following key words:

올린다          편다          짚는다

내린다          굽힌다          뻗친다

## Skim Reading:

As you read the text quickly, underline unfamiliar words and then *guess* the meaning of the words based on other key words in the sentence.

---

**하루30분 요가건강** • • • • • • • • • • • • • • • • • • • • • • • • • • • • • •

**혈액순환에 좋은**
**물구나무서기 자세**

①숨을 내쉬면서 뒤꿈치를 바닥에 붙이고 엉덩이를 들어올려 八자 모양을 만든다. 무게중심이 팔과 다리에 50:50을 이루게 하고 시선은 배꼽 부분에 둔다.

②양 손바닥으로 바닥을 짚고 오른쪽 다리를 몸과 일직선이 되게 들어올린다. 머리끝과 발끝으로 모인 피를 아래위로 한 바퀴 돌려주고 몸의 부기를 가라앉힌다.

**허리선을 날씬하게 해주는 동작**
①옆으로 누워 왼손은 머리, 오른손은 가슴 아래 바닥을 짚는다.

②오른쪽 다리를 천천히 뒤로 뻗쳤다가 다시 앞으로 뻗치는 동작을 10회 반복한다.

③오른쪽 다리를 위 아래로 천천히 움직이는 동작을 10회 반복한다.

**아랫배살 없애주는 동작**
①두 손은 힘주어 손바닥이 아래를 향하게 하고 숨을 들이마신다. 두 다리를 굽히고 위로 들어올려 10초간 멈춘 자세를 유지한다.

②양발을 위를 향해 쭉 펴고 10초간 정지한다.

③바닥과 다리가 45° 각도가 되게 천천히 내리고 10초간 정지한다.

---

## Intensive Reading:

A. *Reading Comprehension:* Read the text thoroughly and answer the following questions:

1. 물구나무서기 자세는 무엇에 좋습니까?
2. 물구나무서기를 할 때 시선은 어디에 두어야 합니까?
3. 허리선을 날씬하게 해주는 동작에서 왼손은 어디에, 오른손은 어디에 두어야 합니까?
4. 아랫배 살을 없애주는 동작에서 양발을 펴고 얼마나 정지해야 합니까?

B. *Grammar:* Find the subject of each clause and fill in the blanks:

1. 숨을 내쉬_____ 뒤꿈치를 바닥에 붙이_____ 엉덩이를 들어올_____     八자  모양을 만든다.
2. 양 손바닥으로 바닥을 짚_____ 오른쪽 다리를 들어올린다.
3. 손바닥이 아래를 향하게 하_____ 숨을 들이 마신다.
4. 두 다리를 굽히_____ 위로 들어올린다.
5. 양팔을 쭉펴_____ 몇초간 정지한다.

## Post-reading Activities

A. In pairs, one student will describe one of the positions or motions while the other student will accurately perform that pose.

B. Describe poses, stretches, positions or motions of other exercises you know outside of yoga. Write your description. Be sure to include all the steps and a brief explanation, if needed.

## Example 5: What to Do in Minnesota (Japanese, beginning level)

These activities were devised by Miaki Habuka of Macalester College. Miaki had the fine idea of making use of a guide to Minnesota produced in Japanese for tourists from Japan. Since the material (including the layout) is culturally familiar to American students, more attention can be paid to decoding the information; furthermore, since the names, places and so on that appear are American, they are written predominantly in katakana, the syllabic writing system for non-Japanese words, thus providing lower-level students with extensive practice in reading katakana.

It's also worth pointing out that in real-life situations, non-native speakers are more often called on to speak about their own culture than the target culture—for example, when I'm in Poland I'm more often asked about American or British matters than Polish ones; these kinds of materials provide great practice in how one can speak about one's own culture in the target language.

---

### Written Text—Example 5: What To Do In Minnesota

**Topic:** Which event to go to?

**Audience:** Adult students at the beginning level

**Language covered:**

A. Katakana

B. Making suggestions

C. Asking about events

**Preparation**

Give the "Minnesota Guide" to students beforehand. Ask them to read the events section of the guide and to guess what events are included.

**Pre-activities**

1. Ask the students what events are held in Minnesota.

2. Have the students match the events written in katakana with their English equivalents.

**Reading Comprehension**

Ask the students the following questions in English; ask them to answer in Japanese (katakana reading/ pronunciation practice).

1. What is the Minnesota Wild?

2. What is the Marshall Fields Challenge?

3. When will the Minnesota Twins play the Seattle Mariners?

4. Where do the Saint Paul Saints play?

5. Where do I call to get information about the Black Nativity?

**Activity 1: Information Gap**

Give the students an event schedule in which different information is included and have them ask when and where an event is being held.

**Activity 2: Discussion**

Tell the students that they will host guests from Japan. Have each pair of students decide which events to go to.

**Follow-up Activity:**

· Ask each pair of students which events they have chosen, where the event is being held, and when they will go.

· Have the students write down the same information.

ソング・オブ・ハイアワサ・ページェント
アメリカの詩人、ヘンリー・ロングフェローの後期詩「ハイアワサの歌」に基づいたインディアン伝説のユニークな描写劇。ツインシティより車で3時間。
2002年7月19〜21日、26〜28日、8月2〜4日
パイプストーン
(507) 825-3316
www.pipestoneminnesota.com

アップタウン・アート・フェア
500以上のアーティストが参加する中西部で最大のアート・ショー。フード、コンサート。子供向けのイベントも。
2002年8月2〜4日
レイク・ストリートとサウス・ヘネピン・アベニュー、ミネアポリス・アップタウン
(612) 823-4581
www.uptownartfair.com

ミネソタ・ルネッサンス・フェスティバル
16世紀にタイムスリップしたようなユニークなフェスティバル。
2002年8月18日〜9月30日（週末のみ）
スカビー
1-800-966-8215（国内フリーダイヤル）
www.renaissancefest.com

ミネソタ・ステート・フェア
700以上のパフォーマンス、300以上の飲食店。ミネソタ博物館の展示、馬、牛、肉、豚、家禽、サラブレッドなどの品評会や、地元アーティストによる美術展、バンジージャンプやウォーターライドなど楽しめる施設も満載。アメリカの夏の風物詩でもある大規模展覧会。
2002年7月12〜14日、19〜21日、26〜28日
セントポール
(651) 642-2200

キャプション: ウォルナット・グローブで行われる野外劇「ローラ インガルス ワイルダー ページェント」

## 主なフェスティバルとイベント

ルッキング・フォー・ルーシー
スヌーピーの生まれ故郷で、作者チャールズ・シュルツ氏が生まれ育ったセントポール市内に、今年はピーナッツの人気キャラクター、ルーシー・バンペルトの彫像が9月から見え始めます。
2002年6月下旬
セントポール市内
(651) 266-8542
www.ilovesaintpaul.com

グランド・セレブレーション・パウワウ
ダンス、音楽などが組み込まれたミネソタのアメリカン・インディアンの文化を祝うお祭り。ツインシティから車で1時間。
2002年6月14〜16日
グランド・カジノ・ヒンクリー
1-800-472-6321（国内フリーダイヤル）
www.grandcasinohinckley.com

ジュディ・ガーランド・フェスティバル
「オズの魔法使い」の主演女優、ジュディ・ガーランドの生誕地で行われる。ツインシティより車で3時間。
2002年8月20〜22日
グランド・ラピッズ
(218) 327-9276
1-800-664-5839（国内フリーダイヤル）
www.judygarlandmuseum.com

テイスト・オブ・ミネソタ
独立記念日を挟んで、ツインシティのレストランのメニューの試食を販売する。ライヴ・ミュージックや花火あり。
2002年7月7日
州議事堂前広場、セントポール
(651) 291-5600
www.tasteofmn.com

前頁写真：ミネソタ科学博物館。
(上）ミネソタ・ティンバーウルブズのウォーリー・ザ・ビアック選手。
(右上）ミネソタ管弦楽団の定期公演が行われる。オーケストラ・ホール。
(右下）夜空を華やかに彩る花火。

1827年独立記念日
ミネソタ州の歴史を再現する軍服のバレードや攻防、歌や踊りなどの賑やかなお祭り。
2002年7月4日
スカビー館、セントポール
1-800-966-8215（国内フリーダイヤル）
www.mnhs.org

「夢のかけら」
「大草原の小さな家」の原作者ローラ・インガルス・ワイルダーの物語の野外劇。ツインシティより車で3時間。同時に開催期を楽しむバイオニア・フェスティバルも開催。
2002年7月7〜14日、19〜21日、26〜28日
ウォルナット・グローブ
(507) 859-2174
1-888-859-3102（米国内フリーダイヤル）
www.walnutgrove.org

ミネアポリス・アクアテニアル（水の祭典）
水をテーマにした夏のフェスティバル。パレード、花火、ボートレースなど。大阪市で開催される「御堂筋パレード」と姉妹フェスティバルの友好関係を結んでいる。
2002年7月19〜28日
ミネアポリス
(612) 338-3807
www.aquatennial.org

キャプション: ミネアポリスのホリダズル・パレード
キャプション: セントポールのウインター・カーニバル

---

『ブラック・ナティビティ』
ペナンブラ・シアター・カンパニーが毎年ホリデー・シーズンを飾る黒人聖歌やジャズなど多彩な音楽とダンスでつづるアフリカン・アメリカンのキリスト生誕ミュージカル。
2002年11月下旬〜翌年1月上旬
フィッツジェラルド・シアター、セントポール
(651) 224-3180
www.penumbratheatre.org

ボリショイ・バレエ『白鳥の湖』
世紀のバレエ団による伝統のクラシック・バレエ公演。
2002年12月3、4日
ノースロップ・オーディトリウム、ミネアポリス
(612)624-2345
www.northrop.umn.edu

## スポーツ・イベント

ミネソタ・ツインズ
ミネソタのメジャーリーグ野球チーム。
4月から9月
メトロドーム、ミネアポリス
(612) 375-1366
www.twinsbaseball.com

マーシャルフィールズ・チャレンジ
PGAプロ、トム・リーマンによる毎年恒例のチャリティ・ゴルフ・トーナメント。
2002年8月22〜24日
ラッシュクリーク・ゴルフコース、メーブルグローブ
(612) 866-7833
www.marshallfieldschallenge.org

セントポール・セインツ
『フィールド・オブ・ドリームス』そのままに野外で観戦するマイナー・リーグ・ベースボール。
ミネアポリス
(612) 375-1366
www.vikings.com

6月から8月
ミッドウェイ・スタジアム、セントポール
(651) 644-6659
www.spsaints.com

ミネソタ・リンクス
女子WNBAプロ・バスケットボールの地元チーム。
6月から8月
ターゲット・センター、ミネアポリス
(612) 989-5151
www.wnba.com/lynx

グランマズ・マラソン
第24回目を迎える五大湖の一つスペリオール湖の沿岸を走るマラソン。開催場所はツインシティより車で2時間15分。
2002年6月22日
1-800-438-5884
www.visitduluth.com

スリーエム・チャンピオンシップ
高額賞金が競われるシニア・プロ・ゴルフ協会のツアー・トーナメント。
2002年8月5〜11日
トーナメント・プレイヤーズ・クラブ、ブレーン
(763) 783-9000
www.pga.com

第84回PGAチャンピオン・シップ
伝統的かつ最大の人気を誇るプロトーナメント。
2002年8月17〜20日
ヘイゼルティン・ナショナル・ゴルフコース、チャスカ
(952) 368-2002
www.pga.com

ミネソタ・バイキングス
ミネソタのNFLプロフットボール・チーム。
8月から12月

キャプション: 人でにぎわうアップタウン・アートフェア

ミネソタ・ワイルド
ミネソタのNHLプロ・ホッケーチーム。
10月から翌年4月
エクセル・エナジー・センター、セントポール
(651) 222-9453
www.nhl.com

ミネソタ・ティンバーウルブズ
人気プレイヤー、ケビン・ガーネットが活躍する地元NBAプロ・バスケットボール・チーム。
11月から翌年4月
ターゲット・センター、ミネアポリス
(612) 337-3865
www.timberwolves.com

ジョン・ベア・グリース犬ぞりマラソン
ダルースをスタート地点にノースショアに沿ったコースを走破する犬ぞりレース。
2003年2月
ダルース
(218) 722-7631
www.beargrease.com

ガバナーズ・フィッシング・オープナー
ミネソタ州知事が陣頭に立って釣り解禁をするフィッシング・イベント。
2003年5月
未定
(651) 296-5029

第7回ノースショア・インライン・マラソン
北米の規模を誇るインライン・スケート・レース。今回初めて「ローラー・ワールドカップ」として、世界の強豪プロが参加する。五大湖のースペリオール湖の湖畔を巡る過酷なコース。
2002年9月14日
ダルース
(218) 723-1503
www.northshoreinline.com

ソルハイム・カップ
LPGAゴルフ・トーナメント。
2002年9月20〜22日
インターラーケン・カントリークラブ、エディナ
(952) 927-7424
www.lpga.com

キャプション: メジャーリーグのミネソタ・ツインズ

---

フォークウェイズ・オブ・ザ・ホリデーズ
1840年代から1890年の開拓民の当時のホリデー・シーズンをそれぞれの建物に再現。
2002年11月29日〜12月23日（週末のみ）
ヒストリック・マーフィーズ・ランディング、シャコピー
(952) 445-6901
www.murphyslanding.com

ホリダズル・パレード
楽しくライトアップしたおとぎ話のキャラクターやサンタクロースの山車が華やかにパレード。
2002年11月下旬から12月下旬、ニコレット・モール、ダウンタウン・ミネアポリス
(612) 338-3807

キャピタル・ニューイヤー
ライブ・ミュージックやパレード、花火など家族で無料で楽しめる大晦日から新年へのお祭り。
2002年12月31日
ダウンタウン・セントポール
(612) 920-9054（内線）
www.capnewyear.org

セントポール・ウインター・カーニバル
パレード、コンサート、氷や雪の彫刻コンテストなどが行われる冬のお祭り。
2003年1月24日〜2月2日
ダウンタウン・セントポール
(651) 223-4700
www.winter-carnival.com

### 音楽/演劇/ダンス/アート

マジック・幻惑の科学
マジックのタネを科学的に明かすエキシビジョン。
2002年5月11日〜9月2日
ミネソタ科学博物館、セントポール
(651) 221-9444
www.smm.org

ミュージカル/『エニシング・ゴーズ』
ジャズ名匠コール・ポーターの名曲の人気ブロードウェイ・ショー。
2002年6月11〜30日
オードウェイ・パフォーミングアーツ・センター、セントポール
(651) 224-4222
www.ordway.org

アレグリア/サーク・ドゥ・ソレイユ
ラスベガスやディズニーででも人気のショーを展開する豪華なサーカス・パフォーマンス。サーク・ドゥ・ソレイユの公演。
2002年夏
ワン・プラネット・アンダー・グループ/ヒップホップとコンテンポラリー・アート
現代美術シーンにおけるヒップホップ音楽の影響を徹底展示。
2002年6月14日〜12月13日
ウォーカー・アート・センター、ミネアポリス

ミネソタ管弦楽団サマー・ミュージック・フェスティバル
多彩なゲストアーティストによる音楽祭。
2002年7月12日〜8月3日
オーケストラ・ホール、ピーヴィ・プラザ、ミネアポリス
(612) 371-5600
www.minnesotaorchestra.org

ミュージカル/『レント』
名作『ラ・ボエーム』を元に70年代のニューヨークの若者たちを描くロングラン・ブロードウェイ・ショウ。
2002年7月17日〜8月4日
オードウェイ・パフォーミングアーツ・センター、セントポール
(651) 224-4222
www.ordway.org

ミュージカル/『レ・ミゼラブル』
ブロードウェイでロングランを続ける名作ミュージカル。
2002年8月7〜31日
オードウェイ・パフォーミングアーツ・センター、セントポール
(651) 224-4222

ミネソタ管弦楽団
100周年を迎え、多彩なアーティストを招いた定期クラシック・コンサート。
2002年9月から翌年5月
オーケストラ・ホール、ミネアポリス
(612) 371-5600
www.minnesotaorchestra.org

セントポール室内管弦楽団定期公演
2002年9月から翌年6月
オードウェイ・パフォーミング・アーツ・センター、セントポール
(651) 291-1144
www.stpaulchamberorchestra.org

『ザ・プロデューサーズ』
トニー賞に輝く大ヒット・ブロードウェイ・ミュージカルが初のツアーを開始。
2002年11月22日〜12月7日
ヒストリック・オーフィウム・シアター、ミネアポリス
(612) 989-5151
www.state-orpheum.com

『クリスマス・キャロル』
歌と踊りを交え、心温まる舞台を繰り広げるチャールズ・ディケンズの名作のクリスマス・ストーリー。
2002年11月16日〜12月29日
ガスリー・シアター、ミネアポリス
(612) 377-2224
www.guthrietheater.org

バイキング：北大西洋伝説
スミソニアン自然史博物館によるバイキングの歴史と伝説をたどる展示。
2002年11月23日〜2003年5月18日

キャプション: ミネアポリスには多くの劇場とレストランが並ぶ。
キャプション: ツインシティ・マラソン

---

## ミネソタのイベント

Match the event written in katakana with the English equivalent.

| | |
|---|---|
| ミネソタ・ツインズ | Musical "Les Miserables" |
| ミネソタ・ルーネサンス　フェスティバル | Uptown Art Fair |
| ミネソタ・ステート　フェア | Minnesota Vikings |
| ミネソタ・リンクス | Minnesota Twins |
| セント・ポール　ウインター・カーニバル | St. Paul Winter Carnival |
| ミネソタ・バイキングス | Looking for Lucy |
| ミュージカル／「レ・ミゼラブル」 | Taste of Minnesota |
| アップタウン　アート・フェア | Minnesota Renaissance Festival |
| テースト・オブ・　ミネソタ | Minnesota Lynx |
| ルッキング・フォー　ルーシー | Minnesota State Fair |

**What Activity/Event To Go To Worksheet**

### Activity 1

Work in pairs. You and your partner have different information. In Japanese, ask your partner for the information that you don't have regarding when and where each event is being held. Then write down the information that you have received in the box.

**Example**

A:＿＿＿＿＿＿は どこで ありますか

B: ＿＿＿＿＿＿＿で あります。

A: いつからですか。

B: ＿＿＿＿＿＿＿からです。

A: いつまで ですか。

B: ＿＿＿＿＿ まで です。

| Event | Where | When |
|---|---|---|
| ＊ミネソタ・ステート・フェア | | |
| ＊ルッキング・フォー・ルーシー | | |
| ＊テイスト・オブ・ミネソタ | | |
| ＊グランド・セレブレーション・パウワウ | | |

### Activity 2

Imagine you'll be looking after Japanese guests visiting Minnesota. Based on the information you've received, discuss with your partner and decide which event to go to.

**Example**

A: どのイベントに　いきましょうか。

B: そうですね。＿＿＿＿＿＿に いきませんか。

A: いいですね。じゃあ いつ いきましょうか。

A: ＿＿＿＿＿＿ は どうですか。

B: いいですね。

Or

A: ＿＿＿＿＿＿は ちょっと。(for refusal)

＿＿＿＿＿＿ は どうですか。(suggest something different)

### Writing

Write at least three sentences about which event you will go to with your Japanese guests, where that event will be held, and when you will go. Start with わたしたちは (we/including the Japanese guest).

## *Literature as a Language-Learning Resource: Examples*

Many people are afraid of using literature in the language classroom. They think it's too difficult, or they're worried that their own understanding of the text is wrong or inadequate. These attitudes are rooted in the misguided ways in which many of us were taught literature; here, a very different approach to using literature in language teaching will be proposed. It is an approach based not just in theory but in experiences many teachers have had with successful use of literature in the language classroom.

This approach will draw on many of the principles mentioned above. It will emphasize the importance of learners' responses to pieces of literature over "correct" versus "incorrect" interpretations; it will look for interactive ways of using texts; and it will not always treat texts "with respect."

At the same time, as with other kinds of materials, you should search widely for suitable pieces of literature to use in classrooms. While there is merit in the classics of English literature (Keats, Longfellow, Dickens), it's usually better to use more contemporary poetry and prose in language classes, as it tends to be easier for students to deal with. You'll see a number of examples of this in the present section.

### Example 1: A Martian Sends A Postcard Home (English, upper intermediate)

This text makes use of a poem by contemporary British poet Craig Raine. Some years ago, Raine invented "Martian poetry"—a way of describing the world as if by creatures who are seeing it for the first time. This leads to strikingly odd images and metaphors. Martian poetry began with this poem: "A Martian Sends A Postcard Home."

When I said earlier that texts are not sacred, I meant that we can alter them, within reason, for our own purposes. Accordingly, I have altered this text minimally by removing a couple of words and one of the sections. Other than that, the poem is unchanged. This activity, which is aimed at upper intermediate learners, is very simple: The learners have to read the poem, guess the missing words, and figure out what is being referred to in each of the eight sections. Numbers have been added for clarity. (For purists, I'm also including the whole unadulterated text.)

These materials are a prime example of the way in which student interpretations of text can take center stage in the classroom. For the second task—working out what is being referred to in the different parts of the poem—there is no right or wrong answer; the poem doesn't come with a key, and we have only our own powers of interpretation and persuasion to rely on.

A wonderful follow-up activity is to ask the students, singly or in pairs, to write their own Martian poems. These are then read to the other students, who have to guess what is being described. It's remarkable how lively a "listening" activity can be when the texts being listened to have been written by the students themselves!

*Literature as a Resource—Example 1: A Martian Sends a Postcard Home*

**A Martian Sends a Postcard Home**

(i)      _____ are mechanical birds with many wings
and some are treasured for their markings –

they cause the eyes to melt
or the body to shriek without pain.

I have never seen one fly, but
sometimes they perch on the hand.

(ii)      _____ is when the sky is tired of flight
and rests its soft machine on ground:

then the world is dim and bookish
like engravings under tissue paper

(iii)      _____ is when the earth is television.
It has the property of making colours darker.

(iv)      _____ is a room with the lock inside –
a key is turned to free the world

for movement, so quick there is a film
to watch for anything missed.

(v)      But _____ is tied to the wrist
or kept in a box, ticking with impatience.

(vi)      In homes, a haunted apparatus sleeps,
that snores when you pick it up.

If the ghost cries, they carry it
to their lips and soothe it to sleep

with sounds. And yet, they wake it up
deliberately, tickling with a finger.

[…]

(vii)      At night, when all the colours die,
they hide in pairs

and read about themselves –
in colour, with their eyelids shut.

Craig Raine

**Questions for students:**

What is being referred to in each of the sections (i-vii)?

What are the missing words or phrases in sections i-v?

**A Martian Sends a Postcard Home**

Caxtons are mechanical birds with many wings
and some are treasured for their markings –

they cause the eyes to melt
or the body to shriek without pain.

I have never seen one fly, but
sometimes they perch on the hand.

Mist is when the sky is tired of flight
and rests its soft machine on ground:

then the world is dim and bookish
like engravings under tissue paper

Rain is when the earth is television.
It has the property of making colours darker.

Model T is a room with the lock inside -
a key is turned to free the world

for movement, so quick there is a film
to watch for anything missed.

But time is tied to the wrist
or kept in a box, ticking with impatience.

In homes, a haunted apparatus sleeps,
that snores when you pick it up.

If the ghost cries, they carry it
to their lips and soothe it to sleep

with sounds. And yet, they wake it up
deliberately, tickling with a finger.

Only the young are allowed to suffer
openly. Adults go to a punishment room

with water but nothing to eat.
They lock the door and suffer the noises

alone. No one is exempt
and everyone's pain has a different smell.

At night, when all the colours die,
they hide in pairs

and read about themselves -
in colour, with their eyelids shut.

Craig Raine

Example 2: Vacations in Kurpieland (Polish/English, intermediate)

In this activity, the text is treated with even less respect. This is a version of an activity called "The Marienbad Game," devised by Mario Rinvolucri. The poem is a translation of a Polish poem by 20th-century poet Anna Świrszczyńska, also known in this country as Anna Swir.

---

**Literature as a Resource—Example 2: Vacations in Kurpieland**

**Vacations in Kurpieland**

We wander all three of us
village to village, forest to forest
up to our ankles in hot sand.
Best is to walk barefoot.

Father collects from cottages
paper cut-outs, from garrets
he pulls out old paintings.

In the evening
I sleep over a clay tureen
of wild strawberries and milk,
over a hunk
of bread as dark as earth,
from a loaf that weighs
as much as I do.

Anna Swir

The text is put on an overhead projector. The rules of the game are simple: You can remove any word, or series of words, up to a whole line; but only from a single line at a time, and if the language that remains still makes grammatical sense. I've done this numerous times. Students call out their suggestions for lines, words, or phrases to be cut; teacher and students together adjudicate whether the proposed cut is feasible, and if it's accepted the teacher crosses out the word or words with a transparency pen. Half way through the activity the poem might look like this:

We wander ~~all three of us~~
village to village, ~~forest to forest~~
up to our ankles in hot sand.
~~Best is to walk barefoot.~~

Father collects ~~from cottages~~
paper cut-outs, from garrets
he pulls out old paintings.

In the evening
I sleep ~~over a clay tureen~~
~~of wild strawberries and milk,~~
over a hunk
of bread ~~as dark as earth,~~
from a loaf that weighs
as much as I do.

---

By the end, we try to reduce it to six words:

We wander ~~all three of us~~
~~village to village, forest to forest~~
~~up to our ankles in hot sand.~~
~~Best is to walk barefoot.~~

Father collects ~~from cottages~~
~~paper cut-outs, from garrets~~
~~he pulls out old paintings.~~

~~In the evening~~
I sleep ~~over a clay tureen~~
~~of wild strawberries and milk,~~
~~over a hunk~~
~~of bread as dark as earth,~~
~~from a loaf that weighs~~
~~as much as I do.~~

(with apologies to:)

Anna Swir

Though at first glance this may seem a "destructive" activity, it's actually pedagogically very valuable, because it requires thoughtful attention to the grammar and meaning of the language being learned. Each time something is cut, the remaining text has to be read anew for sense and for grammatical correctness. On the way, as in the previous example, students learn that text is not always to be treated as sacred, but can be played with and altered—in other words, they learn that the target language belongs to them as much as to native speakers.

## Example 3: Beauty (Swahili, lower intermediate)

Leonora Kivuva, a teacher of Swahili from the University of Pittsburgh, developed these materials on the theme of beauty. As a point of entry she uses pictures of celebrities from a popular magazine. This leads to a discussion on what (and who) is considered beautiful. In this way the students are prepared for a reading of a Swahili poem by Shabaan Robert, a Tanzanian poet, about beauty.

### Literature as a Resource—Example 3: Beauty

**Lesson Objectives:**

· Enhance the students' ability to speak fluently about attributes and people's physical features.
· Bring out the cultural differences on the issue of beauty, and enhance the students' appreciation and understanding of the target language's culture.
· Build the students' appreciation of Swahili poetry, a rich tradition that is part and parcel of Swahili language and history.

**Pre-reading Activity:**

A.   Students will discuss the attributes and physical features of family and close friends using words like mrefu, mfupi, mrembo, mkali, mpole, mshirikina, mwembamba, mnene, mzee, kijana

B.   Students will discuss what they consider as beauty, using pictures of models and postcards.

1. Nani mzuri au mrembo kwenye picha hizi? *(Who is beautiful in these pictures?)*

2. Kwa nini unadhani ni mrembo? *(Why do you think she is beautiful?)*

**Reading the Poem**

1. The teacher will read the poem twice for the students.

2. Solicit information from them about what they understand so far. Let them express themselves freely in turns.

3. Allow time for silent reading and to ask for more information.

**Questions about the Poem: Comprehension and Writing**

· Mwandishi anafikiri nini juu ya uzuri wa uso? *(What does the author think about beauty of the face?)*

· Mwandishi anataka uzuri upimwe na nini? *(How does the author think that beauty should be measured?)*

· Dunia nzima huendeshwa na nini? *(What usually controls the whole world?)*

· Ni nini kilicho na maana sana kwa vyuo vya dunia? *(What is it that is most important for the universities of the world?)*

**Vocabulary:**

In pairs, look up the meanings of the following words in the dictionary. Is the poetic usage the same as the dictionary meaning? Discuss.

| | | | |
|---|---|---|---|
| Pima | Ajabu | Busara | Tijara |
| Johari | Adhama | Rai | Sera |

**Final Discussion: Groupwork**

Je, unakubaliana na mwandishi? Eleza wenzako kikira zako. *(Do you agree with the poet about anything? Discuss with your group.)*

**UZURI**

Uzuri Wa uso mwema,
Unavuta vitu vyote,
vya macho ya kutazama,
unapopita po pote,
Walakini kwa kupima uzuri wa,
   tabia bora

uzuri kupita kupita huu
katika hii dunia
nawapa msisahau,
Ni uzuri Wa tabia
Ni johari ya heshima duniani
kila mara

tazama! dunia nzima
Huendeshwa na tabia
kama tabia Si njema,
si ajabu kupotea.
Kitu kilicho adhama ni tabia
na busara

Kwa kutengeza tabia,
Rai yangu na fikira
Vyuo katika dunia
Vingekuwa na tijara
kwa kuwa nayo daima sera na
   tabia bora.

*BEAUTY*

*Beauty of the face is attractive*
*It draws to it all objects*
*With eyes to perceive,*
*Whichever it passes by,*
*but in comparison the beauty of*
*character is best*

*the beauty that outshines*
*In the universe*
*I give you to hold fast,*
*It's the beauty of character*
*One's honour is the only true jewel*
*in the world*

*Look! the whole world*
*is conducted by character,*
*If the character is weak,*
*No doubt one will stray,*
*Lucky is the one with character and*
*wisdom*

*Speaking of character,*
*My idea and conviction are*
*That places of learning in this work*
*Would render a laudable service*
*To insist upon discipline and unfailing*
*courtesy*

Shabaan Robert

## Example 4: Aunt Cecylia's Adventure (Polish/English, intermediate)

The text reproduced here comes from a Polish novel about a young boy spending the summer in the late 1930s at a country house owned by a friend of his parents. (For the purposes of the present book I've chosen to use an English translation of the text, and in fact I have used the translation in EFL and ESL teaching.) At dinner one evening the company is swapping tales of narrow escapes, and Aunt Cecylia, an aged relative of the host, tells a story from her youth of how she almost died one winter's night after an accident on the marshes. Rather than offering a single set of exercises, a number of different options are listed for this kind of text.

---

### *Literature as a Resource—Example 4: Aunt Cecylia's Adventure*

Over the roast one of the old ladies, whom they called Aunt Cecylia, recounted a story from her youth. It transpired that she too had almost drowned in a marsh, when as a young lady she had been traveling by wagon all the way to Niemirow to fetch the doctor. It happened one night in March. That evening someone in the manor had accidentally cut his shin with an ax, and it was necessary to summon the healer. Miss Cecylia's father was not at home at the time, while the steward lay drunk in his bedchamber; so the enterprising young woman decided she would bring help herself. However, that night there came a thaw, which could not have been foreseen. The young lady had taken a shortcut across the iced-over marshes, confident that she would reach Niemirow without any problem. Suddenly, under the weight of the horse and cart the ice gave way; there was a terrible gurgling sound under the surface and the cart began to sink into the shifting marsh. The horse was stuck up to his hindquarters, unable to move, and was whinnying in fear. The moon shone indifferently; all about there was silence and the soft rustle of the woods. There was no hope. Aunt Cecylia clambered out of the cart, and by and extraordinary stroke of luck, she found a strong branch within arm's reach. She climbed up the tree and sat like an owl in the leafless top of the young oak, wearing a short mantle, a skirt, and a jacket lined with rabbit's fur. Before her eyes the horse, neighing in desperation, sank into the marsh with the wagon. Before daybreak the frost set in again. The young lady shivered on her branch, preparing herself for death. She was haunted, she said, by the reproachful eye of the horse who had perished in the moonlight, helplessly immobilized till he had disappeared in the billowing, greenish depths of the mosses, water and weeds of the marsh. At sunrise Miss Cecylia was found by people from Nalecz who had been sent out to look for her. Afterwards she spent three days in bed, being treated with juices and mustard compresses.

"I almost died," squeaked the old lady, and took a sip of wine.

"And the farm hand?" asked the boy's mother

"Farm hand? What farm hand? I was alone on the marsh."

"The man who'd injured himself with an ax?"

"He recovered," replied the old lady grudgingly, somewhat offended.

From: *The Shadow Catcher* by Andrzej Szczypiorski; translated by Bill Johnston (Grove Press, 1997).

Here are some possibilities for using this text (a combination of such activities is also possible):

1. Give the students the beginning of the story, up to the word "Suddenly." Also provide the ending: "Afterward she spent three days in bed…". After first working to ensure comprehension of the text they have been given, students work in pairs to write the rest of the story, filling in what has happened.

2. Variations on the above: Give students only the beginning, or only the ending.

3. For part of the story, provide jumbled-up sentences which the students then have to arrange in the correct order.

4. Retell the story from the point of view of the horse.

5. Write a newspaper article based on the incident.

6. My favorite activity for this text was suggested by an English teacher in Turkey during a workshop I gave at Izmir University. Complaining that Aunt Cecylia acts extremely passively in the story, the teacher suggested that a more active approach to solving the problem would be in order. She asked: What would McGyver do? The whole workshop burst into laughter. McGyver is a TV character (evidently popular in Turkey as well as in the U.S.) who frequently gets into tight spots like Aunt Cecylia in the story. However, whereas Aunt Cecylia just sits and waits for help, McGyver always thinks up some ingenious way of escaping. Retelling the story in such a way is a wonderfully creative idea.

## Example 5: "Speak" (Urdu, lower intermediate)

This set of activities around a simple but beautiful Urdu poem by Faiz Ahmed Faiz was developed by Blaine Auer, a teacher of Urdu from Wisconsin. Note the way in which students initially have only one stanza to deal with; this way of giving the text to students not all at once but in stages has much to recommend it, as it makes each individual text less overwhelming. At each stage a little more is added, till by the end of the lesson the students are working with the text in its entirety.

### Literature as a Resource—Example 5: Speak

**Unit Topic:** Urdu Poetry

Open discussion with an introduction to essential vocabulary and some basic questions about poetry and the students' own interest in poetry.

· What is the word for poetry in Urdu? Do you know any other words which can be used for poetry?

· Do you like poetry? Yes? No? Explain.

· Who is your favorite poet?

· What is your favorite poem?

· Who are the most famous poets in your language?

Following is an Urdu poem written by Faiz Ahmed Faiz. Assign a verse to each student and have them first recite it in groups broken up by the stanzas of the poem. The students who receive the most difficult verses receive a glossary and must explain the vocabulary to the other students. Assign numbers to each verse and have students recite in random order. Students will then break up into smaller groups and pinpint unknown vocabulary.

After the instructor has explained the literal meaning of the poem, students will break up into smaller groups to answer these questions:

· Who is the poet speaking to in the poem? Write a response from the perspective of the person who the poet is writing to.

- Pick one word from the poem that describes the poem for you. Discuss in your group why you chose this word.
- Why do you think the poet wrote this piece?
- Convert the poem into a short one scene act and perform it in class.

## Further Exercises:

Read some biographical information about Muhammad Iqbal, Mirza Ghalib, and Faiz Ahmed Faiz, three famous Urdu poets. When you are finished, answer the following questions:

- Based upon what you now know about their lives, which poet sounds the most interesting?
- What did you learn about Urdu poets and poetry that you did not know before?

## Websites

For a history and biography of Muhammad Iqbal
http://salam.muslimsonline.com/~azahoor/iqbal.htm

For a history and biography of Mirza Ghalib
http://www.britannica.com/seo/m/mirza-asadullah-khan-ghalib

For a history and biography of Faiz Ahmed Faiz (This site also includes recordings of the poet reading his work.)
http://www.faiz.com

بول ...

بول، کہ لب آزاد ہیں تیرے
بول، زباں اب تک تیری ہے
تیرا ستواں جسم ہے تیرا
بول کہ جاں اب تک تیری ہے
دیکھ کہ آہن گر کی دکاں میں
تند ہیں شعلے سرخ ہے آہن

کھلنے لگے قفلوں کے دہانے
پھیلا ہر اک زنجیر کا دامن
بول، یہ تھوڑا وقت بہت ہے
جسم و زباں کی موت سے پہلے
بول کہ سچ زندہ ہے اب تک
بول، جو کچھ کہنا ہے کہہ لے

**SPEAK**

Speak, your lips are free.
Speak, it is your own tongue.
Speak, it is your own body.
Speak, your life is still yours.

See how in the blacksmith's shop
The flame burns wild, the iron glows red;
The locks open their jaws,
And every chain begins to break

Speak, this brief hour is long enough
Before the death of body and tongue:
Speak, 'cause the truth is not dead yet,
Speak, speak, whatever you must speak.

Faiz Ahmed Faiz

Translated by Azfar Hussain

## Example 6: Love Compared (Arabic, lower intermediate)

Here's another short but striking poem, this time by Arabic poet Nizar Kabbani; the materials were prepared by Samiha Salib of the Schutz American School in Cairo. While Samiha has chosen a more linguistically-based approach, this arises naturally out of the poem. A nice creative activity is included whereby, as with the Martian poem we looked at above, students write their own additional verses involving contrasting pairs of words. Again as with the Martian poem, these student-written additions can then be read aloud in class for the other students to listen to and enjoy.

---

### Literature as a Resource—Example 6: Love Compared

**Topic:** Analogy

**Objectives:**

- Introducing language via literature (a love poem by Nizar Kabbani)
- Reading poetry with a critical eye
- Locating analogies
- Writing poems creating students' own analogies

**Target Group:**

Grades 11-12 Classical Arabic/Arabic Literature Class

**Pre-reading Activity:**

1.  Pass picture cards of the following to the students
    - cloud and rain
    - lantern and moon
    - branch and tree
    - boat and traveling
2.  Ask students to come up with related vocabulary items and define relationship
3.  "Relationships vary." Discuss.

**Listening Activity:**

- Teacher reads the poem twice
- Students listen and locate the specific relationships
- Class discusses poem through the following questions:

    How is the poet different from the woman's other lovers?

    What point does he want to stress?

    How many times is the word **Should** repeated? Why?

**Writing Activity:**

- Ask students to write their own short poems using "Love Compared" as a guide.
- In pairs, have students discuss poems and relationships of the vocabulary items they introduced in their own poems.
- List vocabulary items on board
- Relationships: branch: tree (branch is part of a tree), etc.
- Introduce the term "Analogy"

- Give a sample sentence that defines the specific relationship between the stem words HAPPY : SMILE
  a. owl : milk
  b. lawnmower : anger
  c. love : elevator
  d. sad : frown
  e. college : intelligence

A good answer for this analogy is d. If people are happy, they smile. If people are sad, they frown.

**Enrichment:**

Locate analogies in the following sentences:

**LIMB : BODY**

a. eyes : view
b. cast : bone
c. branch : tree
d. surgery : injury
e. blade : grass

**METER : DISTANCE**

a. runner : race
b. mile : exhaustion
c. hourglass : time
d. quart : volume
e. summer : heat

الحب المقارن

أنا لا أشبه عشاقك ، يا سيدتي

فإذا أهداك غيري غيمة

أنا أهديك المطر

وإذا أهداك قنديلاً .. فإني

سوف أهديك القمر

وإذا أهداك غصنا

فسأهديك الشجر

وإذا أهداك غيري مركباً

فسأهديك السفر

*LOVE COMPARED*

*I do not resemble your other lovers, my lady*

*Should another give you a cloud*
*I give you rain*

*Should he give you a lantern*
*I will give you the moon*

*Should he give you a branch*
*I will give you the trees*

*And if another gives you a ship*
*I shall give you a journey*

Nizar Kabbani

# Resources

As in the case of many other areas of materials development, as far as reading is concerned there are many more resources available in the field of English as a Second or Foreign Language (ESL/EFL) than in foreign language teaching. This means that teachers often have to do a little bit of extra work to figure out how suggestions relating to English-language texts can be adapted for use with texts in the language they teach. Nevertheless, often the most interesting and creative ideas and suggestions are to be found in ESL/EFL books, and the following books come from that field. Those books that I think are particularly valuable are marked with an asterisk.

Aebersold, J. L., & Field, M. L. (1997). *From reading to reading teacher: Issues and strategies for second language classrooms.* Cambridge: Cambridge University Press.

Bamford, J., & Day, R. R. (2004). *Extensive reading activities for teaching language.* Cambridge: Cambridge University Press.

Carter, R. A., & Long, M. N. (1991). *Teaching literature.* London: Longman.

*Carter, R. A., & McRae, J. (1996). *Language, literature and the learner: Creative classroom practice.* New York: Longman.

Collie, J., & Slater, S. (1987). *Literature in the language classroom.* Cambridge: Cambridge University Press.

Day, R. R. (1993). *New ways in teaching reading.* Alexandria, VA: TESOL.

*Duff, A., & Maley, A. (1989). *Literature.* Oxford: Oxford University Press.

Hadfield, J., & Hadfield, C. (2000). *Simple reading activities.* Oxford: Oxford University Press.

Hood, S., Burns, A., & Solomon, N. (1995). *Focus on reading.* Sydney, Australia: National Centre for English Language Teaching and Research, Macquarie University.

Lazar, G. (1993). *Literature and language teaching.* Cambridge: Cambridge University Press.

*Maley, A., & Duff, A. (1984). *The inward ear.* Cambridge: Cambridge University Press.

*Maley, A., & Moulding, S. (1985). *Poem into poem.* Cambridge: Cambridge University Press.

*Morgan, J., & Rinvolucri, M. (1983). *Once upon a time. Using short stories in the language classroom.* Cambridge: Cambridge University Press.

Whiteson, V. (1997). *New ways of using drama and literature in language teaching.* Alexandria, VA: TESOL.

You may be interested in reading more about the theoretical approaches drawn on in this chapter. The notion of reading as an active process comes from schema theory, a theory of reading based in a great deal of empirical research. Good introductions to some of the theory I have made use of—including schema theory, reader response theory, and other aspects of reading—can be found in the following:

Carrell, P., Devine, J., & Eskey, D. (1988). *Interactive approaches to second language reading.* Cambridge: Cambridge University Press.

Flood, J., & Lapp, D. (1988). A reader-response approach to the teaching of literature. *Reading Research and Instruction, 27,* 61-66.

Grabe, W., & Stoller, F. (2001). *Teaching and researching reading.* White Plains, NY: Pearson.

Koda, K. (2005). *Insights into second language reading. A cross-linguistic approach.* Cambridge: Cambridge University Press.

Krashen, S. (1993). *The power of reading. Insights from the research.* Englewood, CO: Libraries Unlimited.

# Chapter Three
# Using Audio Materials

In this chapter we will consider how best to design materials for listening comprehension. The raw materials for the activities will be drawn from a wide range of recorded materials, from songs and comedy skits to radio news broadcasts and recorded drama. Video materials of all kinds provide excellent listening, but they are dealt with separately in Chapter Four. In this chapter, I begin by emphasizing the importance of listening, and I then summarize what we know about what happens when second language learners listen to the target language. The next section outlines important principles that need to be borne in mind when preparing classroom activities based on audio recordings. This is followed by a series of sample sets of materials for listening comprehension using the principles outlined in Chapter One for various languages and levels of learners. A separate section gives some examples of uses of songs for language learning purposes. Finally, there is a short section on creating your own listening comprehension materials.

## The Importance of Listening

In any language there is a huge range of spoken language forms. It goes without saying that there are many kinds of linguistic forms—formal, informal, and so on. But in addition there are different kinds of voices—female and male, old and young; there are all the possibilities offered by intonation, including many attitudinal states from warmth to sarcasm and beyond; there is the emotional content of spoken language, which can convey love, fear, passion, contempt, indifference, and many other emotional states. And last but far from least, there is the huge question of dialects—all languages have dialectal variations, some of which are quite dramatic (think of all the different kinds of English there are in the world), and often these variations manifest themselves more than anything in the spoken forms of the language—in different vowel or consonant sounds, intonation patterns, speed and quality of voice.

It is crucial that language learners have some exposure to this variation, so that they are aware of it and are able to listen at least to the commonest forms, and to a range of different voices. In the past, even when language teachers have made a concerted effort to talk only or mostly in the target language, it has primarily been their voice alone that learners have heard. The longer this goes on, the harder it is for students to deal with other voices, accents, and ways of talking, especially those that are significantly different from the teacher's. Don't get me wrong—it's extremely important for the teacher to use the target language in class, and it's good that learners have at least one target-language voice that they are familiar with. This is not enough, however, and the huge variety of spoken language—of any language—makes it essential that in addition to our own voice, we expose our learners to other ways of speaking the target language that they are likely to encounter.

An obvious example of this are American and British forms of English, though every language has significant variety. To take two examples from my own work, in the Center for Languages of the Central Asian Region, a Title VI center at Indiana University, important decisions regarding dialect variation had to be taken with several of the languages we work with. For Pashto, we had to include the major dialectal varieties spoken in the east and south of Afghanistan. With Uzbek, Tashkent and Samarkand dialects are so different that this too was an issue we could not ignore if the needs of future users of our materials were to be taken seriously into consideration. With any language, an additional complication is that dialects are not "socially equal"—there is always some snobbery about what is a "better" or "worse" form of the language. (My friends from Warsaw, Łódź, or Wrocław to this day make good-natured fun of my "Kraków accent" in Polish.) This also has to be taken into consideration when teaching the spoken forms of the language.

## How Language Learners Listen

Much of what was said in the previous chapter about reading in a second language also applies to listening in a second language. We can say with certainty that listening in a second language:

- Is an active process: We imagine as much as we actually hear. For example, when working with the William Carlos Williams poem about the fallen flower that we saw in the previous chapter, I often read it aloud to my students without showing them the printed version. When the text is heard, the listener must still imagine the hand and the flower—in other words, actively create the text, and not merely listen to the exact words that comprise it.

- Depends on its purpose: How we listen depends on why we listen. When you listen to the weather report, you're listening out for certain key bits of information—what the weather will be like tomorrow, and how warm or cold it will be. When you listen to a sports commentary to a soccer match, you're listening to follow the action. When you listen to a comedy recording, you're listening for jokes, so you can have a laugh. Each of these sorts of listening results in very different kinds of attention being paid to different parts of the text listened to.

- Tends to focus on meaning, not form: Just as with reading, when ordinary people outside of language classrooms listen to something in a foreign language, they listen for the content, not the form. Usually, they don't notice or they forget the form immediately upon understanding the message.

- Is not only about information retrieval: While we often listen for information, that's not all that's going on. Spoken language contains many messages besides the facts or opinions contained in its content. A person's voice tells us what that person is like, how old they are, where they are from, and what their emotional state is. Sociolinguists and psychologists have long known that the "purpose" of most conversations between friends, acquaintances, and even strangers is not the exchange of information, but the establishment and maintenance of social relations; such abilities are crucial for all language learners.

In addition, we need to acknowledge one other fact: Listening in a second language is very stressful! If we are serious about helping our learners to listen better, we need to recognize this stressfulness and work around it, rather than pretending it isn't there.

Psycholinguistic research into listening in both first and second languages has demonstrated the preceding in great detail; if you're interested in learning more, I provide some references at the end of the chapter.

The huge difference between reading and listening—and the one that we need above all to bear in mind as we design listening materials—is that listening occurs in real time, usually with no opportunity to backtrack or pause; if the listener doesn't understand a particular word, phrase, or sentence, it's gone, and a second later the next sentence is upon her. This is the main reason why listening is a much more stressful skill to acquire and practice than reading, and so great care is needed to create activities that do not overwhelm the learner.

# Principles of Listening Material Design

In this section I'll outline a number of basic principles that can act as guidelines in thinking about designing listening activities.

## *1. Use a Range of Materials and Voices*

As emphasized above, it is extremely important that from relatively early on, learners are exposed to a range of voices, kinds of listening texts, and accents. Of course, this should not be done in a way that is overwhelming for the students—asking them to listen to a heavy regional dialect after only a few weeks of the language will be too much. But at the same time, teachers often have a tendency to "protect" their students by not exposing them to variation of the kind that I mention here. In reality, this is often a misguided kindness. As pointed out above, language variation is a reality, and if we really want to prepare our students for communicative uses of the language they are learning, they must be prepared to listen to, and interact with, speakers of different varieties of the language.

In terms of voices, students should hear men's, women's, and children's voices, from different classes and regions. At the same time, it's important to look at this from the student's perspective, not from that of the native speaker or linguist. What I mean by this is that the students' prime concern is to understand; they may not be interested in dialectal variation for its own sake. Indeed, they may not even notice it! Most low-level English learners I have interacted with can't tell if I'm an American or a Brit; why should it matter to them? For them, the main question is whether they can understand me and whether we can have a conversation together. Likewise, it was only after I had been in the States for several years that I started to notice certain American accents—that people from Minnesota, for example, had a particular way of talking. The main point was that I could understand them. When working with dialect speech, then, don't do any more work on it than is necessary for learners to be able to understand.

Regarding the question of what kinds of materials are suitable, as with reading I encourage you to cast your net as wide as possible. Certainly, the following are all possible sources of listening texts, and indeed have been used as language teaching materials in the past (you'll see some of these crop up in the examples given below):

- radio news
- radio weather reports
- radio journalism
- comedy recordings
- recordings of poetry
- books on tape
- recorded instructions
- famous speeches
- radio drama and plays adapted for radio
- songs
- dinner table conversations

- interviews

- telephone information services

- recordings of phone conversations

- recordings of service encounters (ordering in a restaurant, buying airline tickets, etc)

- lectures

- quiz shows

## 2. You Don't Have to Understand Every Word!

One of the most harmful ideas common in listening comprehension is that students must understand every word of the text. Of course, many students want to know what every word is. But this desire is often largely a product of their previous experiences in language learning—they've come to believe that understanding every word is what is expected of them.

Reality is very different. Any second language learner in any real setting will not necessarily understand every word they hear. As I write this chapter I'm living in Poland; although my Polish is good, whenever I go to a movie there are still parts of Polish films that I don't understand. There's little I can do about this in a real-life setting such as a movie theater—I just make do as best I can.

I would argue that it's essential, not just to design activities that students can do without understanding every word, but to explicitly train them to deal with difficult texts—to help them to know how to make use of cues, make intelligent guesses, and so on. We can do this by consistently giving them activities that can be completed without full "understanding"; by doing this, we can demonstrate to students, rather than merely telling them, that it's possible to function in the target language even when parts of the text are beyond their grasp. (This is, of course, the same principle I suggested when thinking about ways of working with reading texts.)

In any case, these activities are all built around tasks that do not require students to understand the entire text.

And lastly—for those students who really want to know every word, have a copy of the transcript to give them at the end of the class!

## 3. Meaning, Purpose, Response

As with reading, in the case of listening comprehension I will suggest that the three related focuses of meaning, purpose, and response offer fruitful ways of approaching the design of listening activities.

### Meaning

Once again I strongly recommend working on meaning before you work on form. Of course, sometimes it's useful and even interesting to focus on some low-level aspect of pronunciation—elision, some regional accent, or a phonemic distinction that doesn't exist in English. But such things should never be the main purpose of a listening task. Always begin with what the listening is about.

## Purpose

As with reading, listening to understand is not a purpose in and of itself. It begs the question: Why should we want to understand in the first place? Of course, there's a certain sense of accomplishment when the learner first "gets" a spoken sentence or conversation. But it's hard to maintain interest if this is the only motivation.

Rather, there should be a real, non-linguistic purpose for any listening. In figuring out what this can be, it's often a good idea to begin with the question: Why would a native speaker listen to this text? While the purposes of native speakers and non-native speaker learners are not always the same, it's surprisingly rare that any sort of likely purposes for listening are recreated in the classroom, even when it's entirely possible to do so.

Whether or not the learners' purpose is the same as that of a native speaker, they need some real, adult reason for listening.

## Response

A few years ago there was an anecdote about a small boy saying that he preferred radio to television because on radio "the pictures are better." This paradox is possible because, as pointed out above, listening is an active process. A crucial part of this is the fact that listening, like reading, involves a response on the part of the listener. Effective listening activities can draw on this response as an integral part of what is done with the teaching materials. A simple example is that, as we listen to someone's voice on an audio recording, we usually develop a picture of what that person looks like, how old they are, where they are from, and so on. Furthermore, we actively imagine the sights and events we hear about—hence the "pictures" that the little boy found so compelling on the radio. Incorporating such responses into classroom activities increases our engagement with the text and with the process of listening itself, and is to be strongly encouraged. Other examples abound. When we listen to a quiz on the radio, we are involved because we are trying to come up with the answers ourselves before the contestants. Listening to a story or a play, we imagine the locations, develop an affection or a dislike for the various characters, and anticipate what will come next. All responses of this kind can and should be built into our listening activities. Examples are provided below.

Generally speaking, it's important always to remember that the best language learning is personal; and furthermore it involves the learner's creativity. There's no reason why listening should be any different in this regard from practice in the other skills.

## 4. Creating Tasks for Listening

Much has been written recently about "task-based language learning," in which learning is primarily organized in terms of tightly controlled tasks that the learners have to complete, such as giving a classmate directions to follow on a map, or ordering an airline ticket. To be honest, I'm a little skeptical about this as a general approach to language teaching—I don't think it represents a solution in itself to the myriad problems of language instruction. However, task-based teaching does have one extremely useful idea to offer: the importance of building language learning activities around concrete, achievable tasks. A great deal of research has shown that activities are much more effective when the learners have a specific goal in mind.

Tasks should be:

- Specific: avoid vagueness, such as "discuss X" or "what do you think about Y?";

- Delimited: they should have a clear end-point and boundaries;

- Achievable within the time and resource limitations of the classroom;

- Authentic: whenever possible, the learners' task should be the same as, or similar to, that of a normal first or second language user outside of the classroom, and completable without understanding every word in the given listening text.

## 5. Using Transcripts to Support Listening Comprehension

For most of the listening activities you'll do, you will need a transcript of the text. Sometimes this will already exist (as with the text of a play or the lyrics of a song); at other times you'll have to spend time preparing the transcript yourself.

In any case, once you have the transcript the big question is: What should you do with it? Of course, one option is simply to give it to the learners as they listen to the recording. However, this is not only rather unimaginative, but it also is not really helpful in learning how to listen to a second language. What the learners need is to grow progressively better at distinguishing the sounds and meanings of the target language. If they have a transcript in front of them when the recording is played, the chances are that they'll be reading, not listening, especially given the usual emphasis on reading in language classes. Furthermore, even for native speakers it's psycholinguistically confusing to have to listen and read at the same time. For this reason, it's best to have learners only listen when they are listening, and to find other uses for transcripts.

The most useful approach is to ask: How can I use the transcript to support the development of the learners' listening skills?

Examples are given below of language learning activities that use transcripts to attempt to support the learners' increasing mastery in the skill of understanding the spoken language.

## 6. Sequencing Your Activities to Support Listening Comprehension

A last concern, both with listening and with other skills, is how to sequence activities so that one supports the next. It's hard to give concrete advice in this regard, since each listening text requires or suggests a different sequence of activities. But in the examples that follow, the sequencing of activities will be as important as the individual activities themselves.

Generally speaking, commonsense guidelines for sequencing activities include the following:

- Easier before harder: this sounds obvious, but it's worth reminding ourselves—have the learners do easier tasks before they do more difficult ones;

- Shorter before longer: Likewise, generally speaking it's better for them to do shorter tasks before longer ones—this gives a sense of achievement and a feeling of making progress, whereas getting bogged down in a long task at the outset can be highly demotivating;

- Receptive before productive: Though this is not a hard and fast rule, it's generally better to do receptive tasks—those involving listening, reading, or viewing—before productive tasks like writing and speaking.

# Some Sample Listening Activities

Below are a few sample listening activities based around different kinds of text, each which uses authentic materials. I've commented briefly on each one to show how the principles and suggestions given above are enacted.

### Example 1: A Doll's House (Norwegian, intermediate)

This activity was developed by Hanna Zmijewska-Emerson, a Norwegian teacher at the University of Minnesota; it's aimed at intermediate students of Norwegian. The activities revolve around an audio recording by the Norwegian National Theatre of *A Doll's House*, a famous play by Norwegian playwright Henrik Ibsen.

---

**Sample Listening Activities—Example 1: A Doll's House**

**Title:** *"Hvorfor spiser Nora makroner?"* Working with an excerpt from Henrik Ibsen's *Et Dukkehjem*

**Time:**

3 weeks, approximately 1 hour per week

**Level:**

Intermediate

**Preparation:**

Builds on existing vocabulary, with the exception of one word, promotion, which is given to students prior to listening/reading

**Purpose:**

· Fits in with the cultural presentation series

· Offers exposure to the spoken word in dramatic form

· Provides practice in speaking skills while acting out the scene

· Provides practice in dialogue during class discussion

· Gives practice in writing skills in the process of writing a continuation to the scene

**From the pedagogical point of view:**

· This activity is proficiency oriented

· All four modalities are present and ideally there is an equal balance between the receptive and the productive activities

· It is based on an authentic text

· It exposes students to the target culture

· It stimulates students' imaginations and creativity

· It offers a possibility of a meaningful dialogue comparing different aspects of 19th century bourgeois society and modern society

**Reading Material**

For the purpose of this activity, I chose a 3-minute excerpt from *Et Dukkehjem* (A Doll's House). It is assumed that students are not at all familiar with the text.

---

**Listening Material**

The CD used is entitled *Henrik Ibsen. Utdrag fra Radioteatrets dramatiseringer.* It is a collection of extracts from twelve Ibsen plays, approximately 3 minutes each.

<u>Publisher:</u>
Lydbokforlaget AS.
Postboks 135, N-7223 Melhus
Norway
Tlf. 47 72 85 6070
Fax 47 72 85 6090
http://www.lydbokforlaget.no
e-mail: office@lydbokforlaget.no

**Note**

The instructor will read the text to students if the recorded text is not available.

**<u>First Week (1 Hour)</u>**

**Listening**

First, as part of a cultural presentation series, the instructor gives a 5 minute introduction in Norwegian on Henrik Ibsen. He/she will also say a little about the play itself (3-4 sentences).

As a point of entry and a title for this section, the instructor chose a question: Hvorfor spiser Nora makroner? *(Why is Nora eating macaroons?)* Students are expected to answer the question after the third listening. The only new word that the students are given is opprykkstilling *(promotion)*. The instructor will then play the chosen scene to the students 3 times.

The first time the instructor will ask them to focus on basic facts:

>Hvem er det som snakker? *(Who is speaking?)*

>Hva snakker de om? *(What are they talking about?)*

>Hva spiser Nora? *(What is Nora eating?)*

>Hvem besøker henne? *(Who visits her?)*

The second time the instructor will ask the students to guess the relationship between the characters:

>Er Nora gift? *(Is Nora married?)*

>Hva heter mannen hennes? *(What is her husband's name?)*

>Hvem er Fru Linde? *(Who is Mrs. Linde?)*

>Hvem er Rank? *(Who is Rank?)*

The third time the instructor will ask the students to visualize the emotional atmosphere in the room:

>Kan du beskrive stemningen? *(Can you describe the mood?)*

>Er Nora glad for noe? *(Is Nora happy about something?)*

>Hvilken årstid et det? *(Which season is it?)*

>Hvem er det som er bekymret og hvorfor? *(Who is worried, and why?)*

**Speaking**

Class discussion is initiated by the instructor:

Hvorfor spiser Nora makroner? *(Why is Nora eating macaroons?)*

Hva skjedde i familien? *(What happened in the family?)*

Hvem fikk opprykkstilling? *(Who got a promotion?)*

Er familien fattig eller velstående? *(Is the family poor or well-off?)*

Et det noe som Fru Linde håper å få? *(Is there something Mrs. Linde hopes to get?)*

Hvorfor er teksten interessant? *(Why is the text interesting?)*

**Reading**

Students receive the original text at the end of class and discuss any vocabulary questions they might have at this point. There is also the opportunity to point out differences between the 19th century forms (written text) and modern Norwegian (spoken text).

## Second Week (1 Hour)

**Speaking**

As an assignment for the next week, students are asked to prepare the scene for acting. They are divided into groups of 4 (the number of characters). After the performance(s), different approaches and interpretations are discussed.

Sample questions:

What is the relationship between Nora and Torvald Helmer?

Why is money so important to Nora and what does it say about her past?

What is the significance of eating sweets?

Why are they forbidden in the house?

Is Nora herself in the presence of her husband?

Are Nora and Helmer a happy couple?

What does Mrs. Linde notice about Nora?

## Third Week

**Writing**

Students are asked to write a continuation of the story in the same groups in which they performed. Based on the scene that they know:

What will happen to Mrs. Linde?

Will Torvald Helmer help her to get the job?

How will Nora react to her husband's promotion and consequently his higher salary?

Is this marriage solid enough to survive anything?

What might happen if there is a conflict?

The final reading takes place the following week. Student read their respective versions to the entire class. The instructor then reads the original ending to the play. A group discussion follows.

**Excerpt from *Et Dukkehjem (A Doll's House)***

......

**Nora.** Hvad bryr jeg mig om det kedelige samfund? Jeg lo af noget ganske andet,—noget uhyre morsomt.—Sig mig, doktor Rank—alle de, som er ansatte i Aktiebanken blir altså nu afhængige af Torvald?

**Rank.** Er det det, De finder så uhyre morsomt?

**Nora.** (smiler og nynner). Lad mig om det! Lad mig om det! (spadserer omkring på gulvet.) Ja det er rigtignok umådelig fornøjeligt at tænke på, at vi—at Torvald har fået så megen indflydelse på mange mennesker. (tager posen op af lommen.) Doktor Rank, skal det være en liden makron.

**Rank.** Se, se; makroner. Jeg trode det var forbudne varer her.

**Nora.** Ja, men disse er nogen, som Kristine gav mig.

**Fru Linde.** Hvad? Jeg—?

**Nora.** Nå, nå, nå; bliv ikke forskrækket. Du kunde jo ikke vide, at Torvald havde forbudt det. Jeg skal sige dig, han er bange jeg skal få stygge tænder af dem. Men pyt,—for engangs skyld—! Ikke sandt, doktor Rank? Vær så god! (putter ham en macron i munden.) Og du også, Kristine. Og jeg skal også have en; bare en liden en—eller højst to. (spadserer igen.) Ja nu er jeg rigtignok umådelig lykkelig. Nu er der bare en eneste ting i verden, som jeg skulde have en sådan umådelig lyst til.

**Rank.** Nå? Og hvad er det?

**Nora.** Der er noget, som jeg havde en så umådelig lyst til at sige, så Torvald hørte på det.

**Rank.** Og hvorfor kan De så ikke sige det?

**Nora.** Nej, det tør jeg ikke, for det er så stygt.

**Fru Linde.** Stygt?

**Rank.** Ja, da er det ikke rådeligt. Men til os kan De jo nok—. Hvad er det, De har sådan lyst til at sige, så Helmer hører på det?

**Nora.** Jeg har sådan en umådelig lyst til at sige: død og pine.

**Rank.** Er De gal!

**Fru Linde.** Men bevares, Nora—!

**Rank.** Sig det. Der er han.

**Nora.** (gemmer makronposen). Hys, hys, hys! (Helmer, med overfrakke på armen og hat i hånden, kommer fra sit værelse.)

**Nora.** (imod ham). Nå, kære Torvald, blev du af med ham?

**Helmer.** Ja, nu gik han.

**Nora.** Må jeg forestille dig—; det er Kristine, som er kommen til byen.

**Helmer.** Kristine—? Om forladelse, men jeg véd ikke—

**Nora.** Fru Linde, kære Torvald; fru Kristine Linde.

**Helmer.** Ah så. Formodentlig en barndomsveninde af min hustru?

**Fru Linde.** Ja vi har kendt hinanden i tidligere dage.

**Nora.** Og tænk, nu har hun gjort den lange rejse herind for at få tale med dig.

**Helmer.** Hvad skal det sige?

**Fru Linde.** Ja ikke egentlig—

**Nora.** Kristine er nemlig så umådelig flink i kontor-arbejde, og så har hun en sådan uhyre lyst til at komme under en dygtig mands ledelse og lære mere, end det hun alt kan—

**Helmer.** Meget fornuftigt, frue.

**Nora.** Og da hun så hørte, at du var bleven bank-direktør—der kom telegram om det—så rejste hun så fort hun kunde herind og—. Ikke sandt, Torvald, du kan nok for min skyld gøre lidt for Kristine? Hvad?

**Helmer.** Jo, det var slet ikke umuligt. Fruen er formodentlig enke?

**Fru Linde.** Ja.

**Helmer.** Og har øvelse i kontorforretninger?

**Fru Linde.** Ja så temmelig.

**Helmer.** Nå, da er det højst rimeligt, at jeg kan skaffe Dem en ansættelse—

**Nora.** (klapper i hænderne). Ser du; ser du!

**Helmer.** De er kommen i et heldigt øjeblik, frue—

**Fru Linde.** Å, hvorledes skal jeg takke Dem—?

**Helmer.** Behøves slet ikke. (trækker yderfrakken på.) Men idag må De have mig undskyldt—

**Rank.** Vent; jeg går med dig. (henter sin pels i entréen og varmer den ved ovnen.)

**Nora.** Bliv ikke længe ude, kære Torvald.

**Helmer.** En times tid; ikke mere.

**Nora.** Går du også, Kristine?

**Fru Linde.** (tager ydertøjet på). Ja, nu må jeg ud og se mig om efter et værelse.

**Helmer.** Så går vi kanske ned over gaden sammen.

**Nora.** (hjælper hende). Hvor kedeligt, at vi skal bo så indskrænket; men det er os umuligt at—

**Fru Linde.** Å, hvad tænker du på! Farvel, kære Nora, og tak for alt.

**Nora.** Farvel sålænge.

......

From Henrik Ibsen, *Et Dukkehjem* (A Doll's House), Act I

## Using Songs

Songs constitute a particular subcategory of listening materials. Generally speaking, songs are to be highly recommended in language teaching. From a psycholinguistic point of view the rhythm, rhyme, and melody all help learners to remember new language, and to do so in a meaningful context, while from the point of view of culture learning, songs themselves are important parts of the target culture. In addition, songs offer insights into other aspects of that culture.

This said, not every song is suitable for teaching purposes. If we really want to focus on the psycholinguistic aspect of learning to listen to the target language, it's important that the lyrics be at least reasonably clearly pronounced. It's for this reason that I avoid a lot of popular music. The fact is that many native speakers can't understand the words to many rock songs; learning them may be interesting, but the distortions of pronunciation that many songs involve mean that in terms of sheer listening comprehension there is little to be gained from work on them.

When choosing songs to work with in class, it's important to think of both the teacher and the students. When I teach ESL or EFL, I try to work with music that I know the students are interested in (this grows increasingly hard as one gets older!). With English it's easier because most students know English and especially American popular music rather well, even if they don't understand the words. When teaching less commonly taught languages, it's much less likely that students will know the popular singers of the target culture. But this is where the teacher comes in—it's good to take the learners' existing interests into consideration, but it's also good to expose them to things that they would not otherwise encounter. It's always surprising to see how students are really interested by target-language music that they might not listen to were it in their own language. There may be a certain mystique about listening to "exotic" singers and understanding their songs; novelty value also plays a part. Yet in other cases, it's possible to make much more direct contact with students. For example, my colleague Jeff Harlig at Indiana University has used Hungarian rap music in his Hungarian language classes; rap exists in most European and East Asian cultures, and elsewhere.

How can songs be used? In much the same way as other listening comprehension activities. All that was said above can be applied to songs. Rather than repeat it all, here are a couple of examples, with some added commentary.

### Example 1: Halika, Biyahe Tayo! [Come On, Let's Travel!] (Tagalog, beginning level)

These materials were developed by Imelda Gasmen, a Tagalog teacher at the University of Hawai'i at Mānoa, who combines songs and a music video. I've included her material here (as opposed to Chapter Four) because the materials focus more on the song itself than on the video. The song is taken from a tourism website aimed at encouraging domestic tourism in the Philippines; its language is simple, and so it can be used with low-level learners. Along with language input, the song provides some useful cultural information about well-known tourist spots in the Philippines.

## Using Songs—Example 1: Halika, Biyahe Tayo!

**Topic:** Traveling in the Philippines

**Level:**

Beginning to Lower-Intermediate Level

**Objectives:**

· To identify places of interest in the Philippines
· To describe in simple sentences at least five places of interest and things to do in those places
· To share and describe the places they are interested in visiting

**Materials:**

· "Biyahe Tayo" music video
· Flash cards of Philippine sites and names of places
· Philippine map

**Pre-viewing Exercise (5-10 minutes)**

**Whole Class Activity:** Ask students if they have been to the Philippines and if they have, what part of the Philippines they have been to. If they haven't been there, what places have they heard or read about, and where would they want to go? List the names of these places.

Distribute two stanzas of the song that get repeated several times and ask them what the song is all about (students speculate; point of entry).

> Tara na, biyahe tayo
> Kasama ang pamilya
> Barkada at buong grupo
> Para mag-enjoy nang todo.
>
> Halika, biyahe tayo,
> Nang ating makita
> Ang ganda ng Pilipinas
> Ang galing ng Pilipino.

**Small Group Work:** Divide the class into groups of 4-5. Match flashcards of pictures of food and things to do with corresponding places (point of entry into the music video). Then, distribute a handout that has the words/phrases describing the pictures plus names of places. Have students match descriptive words with names of places.

**Viewing/Listening Exercise (20 minutes)**

Watch and listen to PART 1 of the music video "Biyahe Tayo." BEFORE listening/watching, have students fill in the blanks with the given clues.

| | | | |
|---|---|---|---|
| Mayon | Luneta | kulay | napapagod |
| Terraces | pareho | nalulungkot | Zamboanga |

Ikaw ba'y _____ (to be sad)
Naiinip, nababagot?
Ikaw ba'y _____ (to be tired)
Araw gabi'y puro kayod?

Buhay mo ba'y walang saysay
Walang sigla, walang _____?(color)

Bawa't araw ba'y _____ (the same)
Parang walang pagbabago?

Napasyal ka na ba
Sa Intramuros at _____ (where Jose Rizal statue is located)
Palawan, Vigan at Batanes
Subic, Baguio at Rice _____? (famous rice fields in the north)

Namasdan mo na ba
Ang mga vinta ng _____ (a province in the South)
Bulkang Taal, Bulkang _____ (famous perfectly shaped cone volcano)
Beach ng Boracay at La Union?

Watch PART 2 of the music video. *While watching*, complete the phrase/sentence on the left with the correct words/phrases on the right.

_____ 1.  Huwang maging dayuhan          a. sa Siargao

_____ 2.  Mag-diving                      b. Luzon, Visayas, Mindanao

_____ 3.  Bangus                          c. sa sariling bayan

_____ 4.  Mag-rapids                      d. sa Anilao

_____ 5.  Lechong                         e. biyahe tayo

_____ 6.  Mag-surfing                     f. ng ating mga kababayan

_____ 7.  Tara na                         g. Balayan

_____ 8.  Sa mahal kong Pilipinas         h. sa Pagsanjan

_____ 9.  Sa pag-unlad ng kabuhayan       i. ang ganda ng Pilipinas

_____ 10. Nang ating makita               j. Dagupan

Watch PART 3 of the video. *After watching*, arrange the following lines in sequence from 1 to 8.

_____ Umakyat sa Antipolo            _____ Halika, biyahe tayo,
      Nagsayaw sa Obando?                      Nang ating makita

_____ Nakisaya ka na ba              _____ Ligaya at pagkakaibigan
      Sa Pahiyas at Masskara                   Kaunlaran, kapayapaan.

_____ Moriones at Ati-Atihan         _____ Tara na, biyahe tayo
      Sinulog at Kadayawan?                    Upang ating matamo

_____ Namiesta ka na ba              __8__ Ang ganda ng Pilipinas
      Sa Peñafrancia sa Naga                   Ang galing ng Pilipino

## Viewing/Listening:

After watching and listening to the three parts of the song, listen to the whole song again.

## Group Work:

Each group is given a map and the lyrics of the song. Locate the places mentioned in the song on the map.

## Vocabulary/Expressions (10 minutes):

Each group lists five new words or expressions. Each group exchanges lists with another group and figures out the meaning based on how the word or expression was used.

**Grammar Points (10 minutes):**

*Infinitive form of verb*

Identify words from the song that are verbs and categorized according to affixes (-um, -mag-,ma). Construct sentences with verbs from the song starting with the pseudo-verbs (gusto, ayaw, pwede/maaari).

*For example:* Gusto kong mag-surfing sa Siargao. Maaari akong umakyat sa Antipolo.

**Post-viewing/Post-listening Exercise (5 minutes)**

Group work: Take one stanza from the song and change at least five words in it. Sing it in class.

Individual homework: Go online and find a picture of a place you are interested in visiting, print the picture, and then write a one paragraph description about it. Bring it to the next class and share it. (Variation: Do an activity where one person describes the picture and another person/group guesses the place being described.)

---

*Halika, Biyahe Tayo!*

Ikaw ba'y nalulungkot
Naiinip, nababagot?
Ikaw ba'y napapagod
Araw gabi'y puro kayod?

Buhay mo ba'y walang saysay
Walang sigla, walang kulay?
Bawa't araw ba'y pareho
Parang walang pagbabago?

Tara na, biyahe tayo
Kasama ang pamilya
Barkada at buong grupo
Para mag-enjoy nang todo.

Halika, biyahe tayo,
Nang ating makita
Ang ganda ng Pilipinas
Ang galing ng Pilipino.

Napasyal ka na ba
Sa Intramuros at Luneta
Palawan, Vigan at Batanes
Subic, Baguio at Rice Terraces?

Namasdan mo na ba
Ang mga vinta ng Zamboanga
Bulkang Taal, Bulkang Mayon
Beach ng Boracay at La Union?

Tara na, biyahe tayo
Mula Basco hanggang Jolo
Nang makilala ng husto
Ang ating kapwa-Pilipino.

Halika, biyahe tayo,
Nang ating makita
Ang ganda ng Pilipinas
Ang galing ng Pilipino.

From city to city,
Seven thousand and a hundred plus islas
Sa mahal kong Pilipinas
Luzon, Visayas, Mindanao ating puntahan.
Huwag maging dayuhan sa sariling bayan!

Nasubukan mo na bang
Mag-rapids sa Pagsanjan
Mag-diving sa Anilao
Mag-surfing sa Siargao?

Natikman mo na ba
Ang sisig ng Pampanga
Duriang Davao, Bangus Dagupan
Bicol Express at Lechong Balayan?

Tara na, biyahe tayo,
Nang makatulong kahit pano
Sa pag-unlad ng kabuhayan
Ng ating mga kababayan.

Halika, biyahe tayo,
Nang ating makita
Ang ganda ng Pilipinas
Ang galing ng Pilipino.

Nakisaya ka na ba
Sa Pahiyas at Masskara
Moriones at Ati-Atihan
Sinulog at Kadayawan?

Namiesta ka na ba
Sa Peñafrancia sa Naga
Umakyat sa Antipolo
Nagsayaw sa Obando?

Tara na, biyahe tayo
Upang ating matamo
Ligaya at pagkakaibigan
Kaunlaran, kapayapaan.

Halika, biyahe tayo,
Nang ating makita
Ang ganda ng Pilipinas
Ang galing ng Pilipino.

Tara na, biyahe tayo
Upang ating matamo
Ligaya at pagkakaibigan
Kaunlaran, kapayapaan.

Halika, biyahe tayo
Nang ating makita
Ang ganda ng Pilipinas
Ang galing ng Pilipino.

Halika, biyahe tayo...
WOW Philippines...

*Song and lyrics can be found at: http//www.lakbaypilipinas.com/biyahe_tayo.html*

## Example 2: Amsterdam (French, upper intermediate)

This is a ballad by Jacques Brel, the famous Belgian singer of the 1960's. The lyrics of the song are very powerful, as is the singer's voice. When I was learning French in the 1970's I was a big fan of Brel, and learned a lot by listening to his songs. This is my favorite. The exercises included here revolve around each of the first three verses of the song, which has four such verses in all.

The activities here do not represent a whole unit on the song; rather, they show some options for activities that promote the skill of listening itself, including examples of various ways in which a transcript can be used to promote the ability to listen. Certain aspects of these activities are worth noting.

First, observe that the activities are divided into verses—focusing on smaller units at a time allows the students to have more of a sense of achievement, and allows us to work in more detail; and it lets us vary the tasks.

Second, note the way in which different amounts of the transcript are given, and how differing levels of "hints" are provided—for example, providing the number of letters of a missing word. Another way of giving such a hint is to provide the first letter of the words in question.

Third, note that some tasks start during the listening, while others include a preparatory stage before the actual listening, in which learners familiarize themselves with the text and work to actively anticipate what they will hear.

If I were to use these materials in class, I would augment them with activities focusing on the content of the song—its atmosphere, the people it describes, and its poetic language.

## Using Songs—Example 2: Amsterdam

**Verse 1**

1. Each of the four parts of Verse 1 begins in a similar way. Listen to this verse and fill in the four different words that appear in these four parts.

> Dans le port d'Amsterdam
>
> Y a des marins qui _____
>
> ...
>
> Dans le port d'Amsterdam
>
> Y a des marins qui _____
>
> ...
>
> Dans le port d'Amsterdam
>
> Y a des marins qui _____
>
> ...
>
> Mais dans le port d'Amsterdam
>
> Y a des marins qui _____
>
> ...

[On a separate sheet of paper:]

2. Now listen to Verse 1 a second time. Listen for the phrase that rhymes with the words you identified in the previous task. In this transcript, each hyphen represents one letter of a missing word:

> Dans le port d'Amsterdam
>
> Y a des marins qui chantent
>
> Les ----- --- --- -------
>
> Au large d'Amsterdam
>
> Dans le port d'Amsterdam
>
> Y a des marins qui dorment
>
> Comme des oriflammes
>
> Le long --- ------ ------
>
> Dans le port d'Amsterdam
>
> Y a des marins qui meurent
>
> Pleins de bière et de drames
>
> Aux --------- ------
>
> Mais dans le port d'Amsterdam
>
> Y a des marins qui naissent
>
> Dans la ------- -------
>
> Des langueurs océanes

**Verse 2**

Listen to Verse 2. Put the missing lines on the right side of the paper in the order which they appear in the song:

i. Dans le port d'Amsterdam

ii._____

iii. _____

iv. _____

v. Ils vous montrent des dents

vi. _____

vii._____

viii. _____

ix. Et ça sent la morue

x. _____

xi. _____

xii. _____

xiii. Puis se lèvent en riant

xiv. _____

xv. _____

xvi. _____

a. Que leurs grosses mains invitent

b. A croquer la fortune

c. Sur des nappes trop blanches

d. Jusque dans le cœur des frites

e. A décroisser la lune

f. Et sortent en rotant

g. A bouffer des haubans

h. Des poissons ruisselants

i. Dans un bruit de tempête

j. Y a des marins qui mangent

k. A revenir en plus

l. Referment leur braguette

**Verse 3**

Look at the transcript below. Now that you know the general atmosphere and subject matter of the song, can you come of up with words that fit the gaps before you listen to it? (Note: Some of the words may be repeated.) Do this in pairs; then listen to the third verse and see whether you were right.

Dans le port d'Amsterdam

Y a des marins qui _____

En se frottant la panes

Sur la panse des _____

Et ils tournent et ils _____

Comme des soleils crachés

Dans le _____ déchiré

D'un _____ rance

Ils se tordent le cou

Pour mieux s'entendre _____

Jusqu'à ce que tout à coup

L'_____ expire

Alors le geste grave

Alors le _____ fier

Ils ramènent leur batave

Jusqu'en pleine _____.

**Amsterdam**

Dans le port d'Amsterdam
Y a des marins qui chantent
Les rêves qui les hantent
Au large d'Amsterdam
Dans le port d'Amsterdam
Y a des marins qui dorment
Comme des oriflammes
Le long des berges mornes
Dans le port d'Amsterdam
Y a des marins qui meurent
Pleins de bière et de drames
Aux premières lueurs
Mais dans le port d'Amsterdam
Y a des marins qui naissent
Dans la chaleur épaisse
Des langueurs océanes

Dans le port d'Amsterdam
Y a des marins qui mangent
Sur des nappes trop blanches
Des poissons ruisselants
Ils vous montrent des dents
A croquer la fortune
A décroisser la lune
A bouffer des haubans
Et ça sent la morue
Jusque dans le cœur des frites
Que leurs grosses mains invitent
A revenir en plus
Puis se lèvent en riant
Dans un bruit de tempête
Referment leur braguette
Et sortent en rotant

Dans le port d'Amsterdam
Y a des marins qui dansent
En se frottant la panse
Sur la panse des femmes
Et ils tournent et ils dansent
Comme des soleils crachés
Dans le son déchiré
D'un accordéon rance
Ils se tordent le cou
Pour mieux s'entendre rire
Jusqu'à ce que tout à coup
L'accordéon expire
Alors le geste grave
Alors le regard fier
Ils ramènent leur batave
Jusqu'en pleine lumière

Dans le port d'Amsterdam
Y a des marins qui boivent
Et qui boivent et reboivent
Et qui reboivent encore
Ils boivent à la santé
Des putains d'Amsterdam
De Hambourg ou d'ailleurs
Enfin ils boivent aux dames
Qui leur donnent leur joli corps
Qui leur donnent leur vertu
Pour une pièce en or
Et quand ils ont bien bu
Se plantent le nez au ciel
Se mouchent dans les étoiles
Et ils pissent comme je pleure
Sur les femmes infidèles
Dans le port d'Amsterdam
Dans le port d'Amsterdam.

### Example 3: Sulunatuuq (Inupiaq, beginning level)

These materials were devised by Andrea Gregg, a teacher at Nikaitchuat Ilisagviat in Kotzabue, Alaska, for use in an Inupiaq elementary language immersion classroom. It is unusual, but appropriate where an indigenous language still used in the community, to make use of a song that students may already know. The song is "Sulunatuuq anilanatuuq," or "What do I want to be when I grow up?" As Andrea states in her footnote, the class would be conducted entirely in the target language. Andrea initially produced the materials in English so that other workshop participants could benefit from them. Note the use of pictures of animals to supplement and the children's learning experience.

## *Using Songs—Example 3: Sulunatuuq*

**Singing**

Sing the song Sulunatuuq with the children (most of the children in this class already know the song).

**Discussion**

What is *amaguq?* What sound does it make? What does it look like?

What is *kayuktuq?* What sound does it make? What does it look like?

What is *tulugaq?* What sound does it make? What does it look like?

Hand out the song with the words and cartoon pictures. Sing the song again. Encourage the children to follow along with their finger as you sing.

Show the real pictures of the animals. Have the students compare the cartoon pictures and the real pictures. What is the same? What is different? Do animals really smile? Which pictures do they like more? Why?

**Writing**

Distribute the "Sua Una?" (*"What is This?"*) worksheet. Let them fill in the blanks. (Uvva una_____. *This is a _____.*)

**Sharing**

Encourage them to sing this song to their parents or grandparents at home. Did their family recognize this song? Was it the same as they remembered or different? Who taught the song to them? Share this information with the class.

Field Trip: Sing this song to elders on weekly trip to Senior Center.

Amaguq: Wolf

Kayuktuq: Fox

Tulugaq: Raven

**Sua Una?**

Uvva una _____.

Uvva una _____.

Uvva una _____.

---

**Song: Suluunatuuq Anilanatuuq** *(What do I want to be when I grow up)*

Suluunatuuq anilanatuuq,

Suluunatuuq anilanatuuq,

Amaguguqlanatuq anilanatuuq.....Owwwwwwww

Suluunatuuq anilanatuuq,

Suluunatuuq anilanatuuq,

Kayuktuguqlanatuq anilanatuuq.....Vaaaaa

Suluunatuuq anilanatuuq,

Suluunatuuq anilanatuuq,

Tulugaquqlanaqa anilanatuuq......Qaaaaa

*\* This entire activity is conducted in the Inupiaq language. No translations are allowed on the teacher's part. Students are allowed to speak English, but are encouraged to speak as much Inupiaq as the are capable and comfortable with.*

## Example 4: Folk Song (Vietnamese, beginning level)

These deceptively simple materials are the work of Nguyen Phuong of Lansing Community College in Michigan. They make use of a traditional Southern Vietnamese folk song involving call and response. This short text, which can be sung by the teacher or played from a recording, is extremely evocative of a very particular place and activity, and contains a great deal of cultural information. Phuong further engages the students by encouraging them to follow this song by creating their own call-and-response songs in the same style.

### Using Songs—Example 4: Vietnamese Folk Song

**Topic:** Folk Songs

**Level:**

Intermediate

**Objectives:**

1. Recognition of a type of poetry
2. Appreciation of national heritage poetry
3. Improvisation of similar songs

**Introduction:**

The importance of oral tradition which leads to formal poetry.

**Tasks:**

1. Have students listen to the poem without seeing the text. Afterwards, ask them to visualize the setting and to describe the circumstances (who, what, when, where). Solicit responses from students regarding the vocabulary, style, and dialect.
2. Read the poem aloud for pronunciation. What vocabulary helps to establish the scene, gender of the speakers, circumstances, dialect, and mood?
3. Ask students to write a response to the 2nd couplet, and also a reply to the response.
4. Discuss with the class the origin of folk songs, their purposes, the ease or difficulty of improvising such songs, and when they are used (e.g., to lighten workloads, to start friendships, as a means of friendly teasing, for village contests, or the sheer joy of it).
5. Hands-on application and practice: Have students work in pairs or male/female groups to create/improvise a song in similar fashion to other settings of the students' liking (e.g., walking on campus, asking for a date in a poetic tone, etc.). Ask students to give oral interpretations of their masterpieces.

---

**Folk Song: Southern style**

Male voice: Hò ơ....hò Chớ bố ghe ai chèo mau anh đợi ơ ơ...
Chớ kẻo giông tới rồi...hò ơ...mà trời lại tối tăm ơ....
*(Hey there...whose boat is lagging behind...hurry up...I'm waiting for you*
*But the storm is coming soon...hey there...and the sky is getting dark...)*

Female voice: Hò ơ...Bố ghe ai mà chờ đợi em cùng....
Chớ ghe em mà chở nặng chớ lạnh lùng mà khó đi hò ơ....
*(Whose boat is it ahead...please wait for me...I'm coming along*
*But my lone boat is laden and heavy...and I'm rowing with difficulty...)*

# Afterthought: Making Your Own Recordings

When I worked in Poland in the early 1980's, my colleagues and I had very little in the way of good materials, and it was very hard to get anything new. The situation forced us to be resourceful. One of the things we did was to create our own listening materials. We used our own voices, including those of both native and non-native speakers, and created texts and activities that were rather rough-sounding and amateurish, but on the other hand were personalized and geared to the needs and interests of our particular learners. Though this is not an ideal solution, for many teachers (and learners) it can be an enjoyable and effective way of increasing the range of listening materials you have available. Following are two such examples of "home-made" materials.

## Example 1: United States/Great Britain Differences (English, lower intermediate)

This material arose when I was teaching on a residential course with two American teachers, and our learners became curious about the differences between British and American English. We didn't have any suitable materials on hand, so my American colleague Tom Patterson and I put together the following text and exercise. It's not particularly imaginative, but it was fun to do, and the learners enjoyed it immensely!

---

### *Making Your Own Recordings—Example 1: U.S./G.B. Differences*

**United States/Great Britain Differences: Worksheet**

**Level:** Lower Intermediate

*Oscar Wilde described Britain and America as "two countries divided by a common language." Here's what he meant...*

**1. First Listening:** Listen to the conversation on the tape.

A.  Where does this conversation take place?

B.  Who are the speakers?

C.  List four examples of misunderstandings between the speakers:

1. _____   3. _____

2. _____   4. _____

**2. Second listening:** Listen to the recording again. This time, complete the following pairs of terms in British and American English:

|    | United States | Great Britain |
|----|---------------|---------------|
| 1. | sidewalk      | _____ |
| 2. | parking lot   | _____ |
| 3. | _____ | city center   |
| 4. | _____ | boot          |
| 5. | gear shift    | _____ |
| 6. | _____ | tram          |
| 7. | subway        | _____ |
| 8. | _____ | cheerio       |

**3. Third listening:** Listen one more time to the whole recording. What differences do you notice between American and British pronunciation? List as many of these as you can.

**U.S./G.B. Differences: Transcript**

BILL: Excuse me, this is a garage [pron. *garridge*], isn't it?

TOM: You mean, a garage [pron. *garahdge*]?

BILL: Yes.

TOM: Yeah.

BILL: Good, I need some help. You see, my car's broken down.

TOM: What's the problem?

BILL: Well, we were just on our way to the city centre when—

TOM: To the where?

BILL: To the city centre—the centre of the city.

TOM: Oh, you mean downtown. OK, go on.

BILL: Yeah. Anyway, and the gear lever just sort of came off in my hand.

TOM: Um, the gear shift, you mean?

BILL: Yes, that's right, I think so.

TOM: So what kind of car is it?

BILL: It's a Ford.

TOM: Sedan or station wagon?

BILL: What?

TOM: Does it have extra room for luggage in the back?

BILL: Oh, I see. No, it's a saloon car, not an estate.

TOM: OK, sedan. Where is it now?

BILL: Well, I couldn't find a car park anywhere, so—

TOM: You mean a parking lot?

BILL: Yes, that's right. So I had to park it right here, just on the pavement.

TOM: The what?

BILL: On the pavement. You know, by the side of the road, where people walk.

TOM: Oh! The sidewalk.

BILL: Yes. Anyway, I'd be very grateful if you could come and have a look at it.

TOM: Well, I haven't got a spare gear shift right now, but if you come back later this morning it'll be fixed.

BILL: OK, thanks. But actually, do you think you could give me some more petrol while you're mending it?

TOM: You mean gas? Sure. But don't leave anything in the trunk.

BILL: In the what? Oh, you mean the boot. No, it's OK, it's empty. But can you tell me how I can get into the city?

TOM: All kinds of ways. Let's see. You could take the streetcar—

BILL: You mean the tram?

TOM: Yep. Or the subway.

BILL: Underground?

TOM: Yep. Or there's even a local train from the railroad depot.

BILL: The railway station, that is?

TOM: Um, yep.

BILL: Aha, I see. Thank you very much. I'll call back later this morning.

TOM: No trouble at all.

BILL: Cheerio!

TOM: Have a nice day!

BILL: (to himself) Strange chap. . .

TOM: (to himself) What a weird guy. . .

## Example 2: Guided Fantasy (English)

This example, which can be either recorded, read, or spoken, began as part of a theatrical exercise for a course in theater that I taught for teenage ESL students. I've since used it successfully with various groups of learners. This is a prime example of the importance of learner imagination and creativity in responding to listening texts.

---

### *Making Your Own Recordings—Example 2: Guided Fantasy*

**The Time Machine**

Close your eyes and find a comfortable position to sit in. All you have to do is listen to me.

Imagine that you have been put in a time machine, and that for a short while you can go back to any period in history that you choose, and any place. Decide now which period you want to visit, and which place.

[pause]

The machine starts. You are traveling back . . . You have arrived. You get out. What can you see? Are there any buildings? What are they like? There are people around. How are they dressed? You start walking. What are you walking towards? Some people come up to you. What happens next?

[pause]

Now, unfortunately, you have to return to the time machine. How do the people react? You walk back slowly to the machine and climb in. Everyone watches. What are they doing?

The machine starts . . . now you have come back to the twenty-first century, to your classroom. When you are ready, open your eyes.

[pause]

Now, write the story of your journey into the past. Write about what you saw, the people you met, and the things that happened to you.

---

# Further Reading

If you are interested in reading more about the psychology of second language listening, two good sources are:

Rost, M. (1991). *Listening in language learning.* London: Longman.

Rost, M. (2005). L2 listening. In E. Hinkel (Ed.), *Handbook of research in second language teaching and learning* (pp. 503-527). Mahwah, NJ: Lawrence Erlbaum Publishers.

The following books contain useful information and ideas about the teaching of listening:

Buck, G. (2001). *Assessing listening.* Cambridge: Cambridge University Press.

Flowerdew, J., & Miller, L. (2005). *Second language listening: Theory and practice.* Cambridge: Cambridge University Press.

Mendelsohn, D. J. (2000). *Learning to listen.* White Plains, NY: Dominie Press.

Mendelsohn, D. J., & Rubin, J. (Eds.). (1995). *A guide for the teaching of second language listening.* White Plains, NY: Dominie Press.

Rost, M. (2001). *Teaching and researching listening.* White Plains, NY: Pearson.

Ur, P. (1984). *Teaching listening comprehension.* Cambridge: Cambridge University Press.

The following books all offer valuable ideas for creating listening activities in the classroom:

Davis, P., & Rinvolucri, M. (2002). *Dictation: New methods, new possibilities.* Cambridge: Cambridge University Press.

Hadfield, J., & Hadfield, C. (2000). *Simple listening activities.* Oxford: Oxford University Press.

Murphey, T. (1994). *Music and song.* Oxford: Oxford University Press.

Nunan, D., & Miller, L. (1996). *New ways in teaching listening.* Alexandria, VA: TESOL.

White, G. (1999). *Listening.* Oxford: Oxford University Press.

# Chapter Four
# Using Video Materials

## Introduction

It has been said that civilization as a whole is in the process of shifting its fundamental preference for the way in which it gathers information, away from a reliance on written sources and towards visual media such as film and television. In reality this position is a bit of an exaggeration—a great deal of Internet use, for instance, depends on intensive reading and writing. Many young people, including many students in our LCTL classes, would, given the choice, watch a film rather than read a book. For this reason if for no other, it is worth thinking about using video materials in our classrooms. But there are other, strong pedagogical reasons for using video. Video shows language in use; unlike audio recordings, it can help the students with contextual clues based on facial expressions, gestures and so on; and it can provide fascinating cultural information about what places look like—rooms, houses, streets, and institutions in the countries and regions where the languages we teach are spoken.

This chapter offers some guidelines for incorporating video in language teaching, and includes some examples of projects in a few different languages.

One note: the word "video" is used here as a form of shorthand for recorded moving images. The exact form the recording takes is not relevant—it could be DVD, laser disk, or a "traditional" VCR tape. The technical way in which scenes are marked and played will differ, but the pedagogical principles of their use do not change.

These principles in fact closely resemble the ones I recommend in Chapter Two discussing the use of written texts. Let's summarize the principles here:

1. Find a point of entry to get learners interested in the material.

2. Use only the minimum necessary pre-teaching of vocabulary.

3. Focus first on the content of the material.

4. Don't treat the materials as sacred: Make whatever use of them best suits your purposes.

5. Aim for tasks that are interactive and open-ended.

6. Design activities around a specific purpose that can be achieved without understanding every word of the materials.

7. Take advantage of the fact that several people are gathered together in the classroom.

8. Save work on language—vocabulary, grammar and so on—till the end.

9. Try to integrate work on video, which will in most cases primarily revolve around listening, with other materials and other skills (reading, speaking, writing).

# How Language Learners Watch Video

If we are to design good viewing materials, we need first of all to take into consideration what we know about how second language learners go about watching film and television. In this section I outline some of what research and experience has taught us about this.

First, just as with writing and audio listening, viewing is above all an active process. In other words, when we watch, we are simultaneously constructing hypotheses about the meaning of the language and the visual information we see. When watching a film, we are anticipating how the story will develop, speculating on why the characters act as they do, and guessing at the significance of details we see and hear. As we watch a situation comedy (a sitcom), we often laugh because the characters do exactly what we don't expect—but it is only because we are actively anticipating what they *will* do that the element of surprise (and thus comedy) is possible. At other times in the same sitcoms, we laugh because the characters do just what we suspect they will do but hope they won't, because it's obviously a disastrous choice of action; but again, it's precisely the fact that we can foresee both their actions and the consequences of those actions that makes the comedy possible. The same applies to the words characters use—as with written forms of language, we actively anticipate how phrases, sentences, and dialogues will continue, and even when we're surprised, it's still our ability to predict that makes us capable of laughing at the unexpected.

In all these things, second language learners are no different. They may not initially be able to pick up on cultural clues in movies, or know the characters in sitcoms, but at all times they are actively working to make sense of what they see. And, as with writing, the best uses of video materials draw on these active processes and turn them into opportunities for both receptive and productive language use.

The mention of cultural clues reminds us of another important aspect in the way second language learners take in video. Each culture has its own visual language with special meanings for particular gestures, facial expressions, intonations and so on. It may be here that learners need the most help. Without guidance, they may have trouble understanding the significance of the ways in which characters interact on screen, or they may misinterpret them without realizing it, for example assuming two characters are arguing when in fact they're just conversing. At the same time, such aspects of communication remind us of the rich possibilities inherent in video, and point the way to many useful and engaging activities.

As was the case with listening, it's also vital to remember how stressful it is to watch native speakers speaking. Speaking on video happens in real time, and, unlike the written word, it's immediately followed by more speech. It often feels that, if you miss one word, there's no time to stop: like a person who trips in a quickly moving crowd of people, one slip and you fall under. Furthermore, different speakers of any language will vary widely in accent, voice quality and other characteristics. In many cases the language used will not match exactly what is in the learners' coursebook, or the video's sound recording may not be of the highest quality. All these factors mean that listening to video can be a nerve-wracking experience, especially for students whose previous language learning endeavors has led them to believe they need to understand every single word.

Does this mean we should stop using video? I would argue quite the opposite—that precisely because of these difficulties, it is *essential* to work as much as possible with video and audio materials. The shock of hearing the target language used naturally—that is, quickly and colloquially—is going to come sooner or later; it's best to get it over with right from the beginning, and get students accustomed to listening to native speakers from the very first classes. In connection with this, though, two interconnected things are essential: as before, learners have to get comfortable with the idea of not understanding every word; and they need to be given tasks that can be completed with only a partial understanding.

## What Kinds of Video Can Be Used?

In previous chapters, I encouraged you to be open to the possibility of using many different kinds of materials; I suggested that a good starting point in selecting materials is to think about the learners' own interests and preferences. The same advice applies to the selection of video. Some of the different kinds of recorded video materials that I have used myself, or seen others use effectively, include the following. This is by no means an exhaustive list, but only indicates the possibilities.

- Feature films

- TV News

- Situation comedies

- Television documentaries

- Television commercials

- News magazines (e.g., *Dateline*)

- Soap operas

- Quiz shows

- Variety shows

- Comedy sketch shows (e.g., *Saturday Night Live*)

- Recordings of plays

- Silent movies

## Making Your Own Videos

It is also entirely possible to make one's own videos; I've done this myself, and have seen others do it successfully, and I shall include a couple of examples of this kind of video in this chapter. Shooting your own videos obviously gives a whole range of additional possibilities, amongst them the chance to show authentic cultural contexts in which your language is spoken. Furthermore, in some countries little is commercially available in the way of contemporary video; in others, legal restrictions make it difficult to get hold of good material. In such cases, making one's own materials can be a useful alternative.

It has to be acknowledged from the outset, though, that such an undertaking can be difficult, mostly from a technical point of view, and it can be very expensive. We are trained as teachers, not as video technicians or camera operators; as anyone knows who has tried it, filming an event is not simply a question of pointing the camera and pressing the record button. It's important not to underestimate the complications of doing your own recordings. Furthermore, you need to bear in mind the legal consequences of filming real people. Anyone who appears in a video, or even in still photos, should sign a release from allowing the developers to publish the images. This is an important courtesy, as well as a legal necessity. This said, however, where the technical and financial resources are available, making one's own videos can be excellent for language teaching. At the Center for Languages of the Central Asian Region (CeLCAR), a Title VI National Language Resource Center at Indiana University, authentic materials have been recorded in-country for all four languages for which coursebooks have been written: Pashto, Tajik, Uyghur, and Uzbek. Examples of materials that utilize these video recordings are included in this chapter; though the source of the raw material is different, the writers have included the same kinds of activities that are recommended here.

# Two Possibilities for Viewing Activities

As a rule, I don't like to make categorical pronouncements about a matter as complex and unpredictable as materials design. Most of the recommendations and suggestions in this book are just that—indications about what, other things being equal, is a good way to think about an issue.

However, in this section I will make such a pronouncement. In my many years' experience of teaching language and working with language teachers, I have found that working with video must involve one of two very distinct kinds of viewing: *extensive viewing,* in which learners view long recordings (e.g. a feature film or a television show); or *intensive viewing,* in which concentrated work is done on a short recording, often an extract from something longer. Furthermore, I strongly recommend that an extract selected for intensive viewing should be no longer than 4 minutes at an absolute maximum, and ideally should be between 1 and 3 minutes long. My reason is simple: it is very disheartening to realize how much of a TV show or movie you do not understand, and how much intensive and difficult work you need to get it. Mastery of a two- or three-minute scene, on the other hand, is possible within the confines of a single lesson, and gives the learners a sense of achievement, an "island of security" in a longer film or program. In this chapter I will be taking the "four-minute rule" as a given in the activities I describe.

The following two sections set out some options for each of these kinds of viewing. More space is devoted to intensive viewing because it is harder to do, more labor-intensive to prepare, but also much more beneficial to the learners in terms of their learning how to listen.

## *Intensive Viewing*

This section begins with an overview of the different components of a set of activities: pre-viewing activities (the point of entry), intensive viewing activities, language work, and follow-up activities. For each component a few ideas and examples are provided. Following this are three examples of completed units in which these components can be seen.

### Pre-Viewing Activities: The Point of Entry

Just as with reading and listening, learners' engagement with video texts will be much greater if you can start by capturing their curiosity or interest in the video they are going to watch. And just as with reading and listening texts, we can think of this as finding a point of entry into the video.

In some cases, as with reading and listening, this can be a title, a single word, or a picture—perhaps a still from the video.

For example, in the clip from "Incident at the Train Station" described below, we took a single sentence from the text and used this sentence as the point of entry. The sentence is (in translation):

> "I knew they'd come for me. I knew I had no escape."

We asked the learners to speculate on who might have said this sentence, to whom, and under what circumstances. (In the video, the man arrested for the murder utters this sentence in an interview from his cell.) This brief activity provided the point of entry.

The point of entry should be something that gets the learners thinking; it should *not* be just a list of words from the scene. As with reading and listening texts, it is not a good idea to give the learners all the new words that appear in the video. Quite the opposite—give them *only* those words that are absolutely essential to complete the first task you give them.

On the other hand, new words can be used *if* they encourage a creative, active approach to the text. For example, we might say to the learners:

Can you imagine how the following words and phrases could all form part of the same story?:

|          |                |       |
|----------|----------------|-------|
| babka    | Saddam Hussein | cane  |
| Gore-Tex | limp           | wine  |

(These words all form part of a single episode of the sitcom *Seinfeld* I have used in teaching.)

This way of introducing new vocabulary is more effective because it requires some active work on the part of the learners.

## Ideas for Intensive Viewing Activities

Many of the ideas for intensive viewing activities resemble those suggested for reading and listening; others arise from the nature of video. Here are some general ideas, along with a few examples. The following ideas relate to individual activities, and can all be used in combination with each other, as well as with the other components described in other sections.

### Sound Off

Video allows us to turn the sound off and watch only the images. I'm always amazed when I do such an activity to see how much the lack of sound forces viewers to concentrate and watch very intently. There are many possible uses for soundless video viewing: predicting what is going on, guessing what the speakers' voices are like, guessing what the commentary may be (for example with a travelogue), and so on. All these kinds of activities help to prepare students for what they will subsequently hear, encouraging them to anticipate actively the language that will be heard from the video which, in turn supports their ability to listen effectively.

### Vision Off

Of course, it's also possible to do the opposite: to cover the screen up and listen without the picture. (Alternatively, you could just use a recording of the soundtrack, though it's more fun to have the television there with a cloth or paper covering the screen!) This activity can involve guessing who the speakers are, what they look like and how they're dressed, where the scene takes place, and what actions are going on.

## Split Screen

Another variation on the above is to cover up half the screen only—you choose which half! Again, the purpose is to engage the students in actively guessing what it is they cannot see, on the basis of the language they hear and cues from the visible half of the screen.

## Selecting a Key Scene

Even if you're aiming at extensive viewing—such as showing a movie—selecting a key scene for intensive work can significantly enhance the experience. A few years ago, as part of evening activities on a residential course, my colleagues and I were showing an old British action movie called *The Italian Job* (a new American version of this film appeared a couple of years ago). The movie mostly involves people chasing around in cars; there's not a lot of language. However, in one crucial scene, about a minute and a half long, the criminal mastermind explains to the leader of the thieves (Michael Caine) what the plan is. This information is vital to an understanding of what goes on in the rest of the film; so I developed a simple gap-filling activity based around a transcript of this scene.

## Recalling a Sequence of Events

A colleague of mine, Colin Campbell, once showed his learners the opening sequence to *Superman II,* a largely language-free street scene in which a series of catastrophic accidents and mishaps are set in motion by a pretty woman walking by. The intermediate-level learners were shown the scene once, then asked to recall (in English, the target language) the exact sequence of events. It was a memory test, but a linguistically demanding one that required them to describe in words all the actions and incidents they had seen on the screen.

## Adding a Soundtrack

Even silent films can be used for language learning! As with pictures (see Chapter Five), a language-free stimulus can be used to provoke creative and imaginative language use by the students. Select a 1-3 minute extract or scene from a silent film. Divide learners into groups of three; give each group a tape recorder and ask them to prepare a sound track for the scene. A variation on this is to use a scene from a film with sound, but with the sound turned off; this is harder, but also more fun.

## Spotting Your Sentence

The point of entry can sometimes be one sentence that you are familiar with. When using a scene with lots of dialogue by different speakers (for instance, a party or a large dinner), give each learner a slip of paper with single sentence from the transcript. Then play the scene; the learners have to wave their slip of paper when they hear their sentence.

## Building Up Backwards

Video, like any other kind of other text, is not sacred. We can work with it in any order we wish. When I used the episode of *Seinfeld* mentioned above, I began with the last scene, in which four people arrive at a dinner party, hand over a cake and a bottle of wine, and leave. Why is this? What is going on? Viewing this unexpected incident led the learners to speculate on what might have led up to it; this was the point of entry to the rest of the episode. From this point we worked backwards, doing work on three or four 1-3 minute scenes, till the learners knew enough to be able to watch and appreciate the whole program. A 24-minute show thus occupied about two hours of class time.

Using Transcripts

Transcripts of video materials can be used in much the same way as audio transcripts—in other words, all the suggestions given in Chapter Three can be employed when working with video. Examples of such activities are included in the sample materials offered below.

## Working with Language

Working with transcripts of a soundtrack, one can do the same kinds of language work that we have already seen in the chapters on reading and listening—drawing attention in various ways to aspects of grammar or vocabulary. For example, in the unit about the murder at the Polish railway station we included an activity designed to focus on common collocations used in discussing crime (see below).

But use of transcripts with video also offers rich possibilities for focusing on other aspects of language. Because video shows facial expressions, body language, and gestures, as well as the words used, we get more of the "full experience" of using the language than is possible on an audio tape or in a written text. For example, one activity I have used calls the learners' attention to the fillers that we insert between sentences to indicate attitude, manage the discourse and so on. This was done on the basis of an episode of the British comedy series *Fawlty Towers;* I provided a transcript that included all the "content" of the dialogue but had gaps wherever characters said "uh," "ah," "oh," "well," and other such expressions, which contain no propositional information but which serve other purposes such as structuring discourse, conveying attitude, and so on.

Two colleagues in the Intensive English Program at Indiana University, Mindy Uhrig and Corey Muench, have used scenes from the American TV situation comedy *Friends* to demonstrate the importance of intonation. For example, in one episode the characters are locked out of an apartment because one of them hears the question "[have you] got the keys?" as a statement "[I've] got the keys." Whether or not intonation involves misunderstanding, it's always a crucial aspect of language, and each language has its own intonational conventions. Video offers a rich source of information about, and examples of, this area of language.

Whatever aspect of language is looked at, the experience of *seeing* people using particular kinds of intonation, fillers, turn-taking, etc., is infinitely more interesting, memorable, and convincing than simply being told by your teacher that such things exist.

A word of warning is in order though, because the "authenticity" of some forms of language and discourse found on commercial television and in films is questionable. Such media create their own norms, which should not be mistaken for the kind of language actually used between "ordinary" people in real life. For instance, in real conversations there are often quite elaborate sequences known as pre-closings and closings that we use to prepare to end a conversation and then to actually end it. In films, such sequences rarely appear, because screenwriters need to keep things to a minimum, and because they employ the language of film, not that of real life. In films, people often don't even say "goodbye"! So we need to be careful in this regard. On the other hand, film and especially television dialogue is often pronounced very clearly, and so is easier to follow than authentic language from interviews and other kinds of news television. This is especially true for intermediate learners.

*Follow-up Activities*

It goes without saying that the full range of follow-up (post-viewing) activities can be considered for video as well as audio materials. A couple of years ago, a TV ad for the NBC television station showed an ESL class performing an episode of the hospital drama *ER,* using board erasers to represent a defibrillator. This kind of "acting out" can be great fun as a post-viewing activity, especially if the learners create their own dialogues; for such performances learners often like to be taped. Many different kinds of activities can be imagined, and two primary directions can be considered for such activities:

1.  Those activities aimed at re-using and thus reinforcing the specific language used in the video, while at the same time possibly extending it in some way.

2.  Those activities that stimulate personal and/or creative responses to situations, characters, or issues raised in the video.

Of course, many activities will do both. However, it can be helpful to think of these in principle as two distinct possibilities.

## Using Video: Sample Materials

In this section we'll take a look at examples of video-based materials. As always, the purpose of these examples is not to show how things *should* be done, but how they *can* be done.

### Example 1: Incident at the Train Station (Polish, upper intermediate)

These materials were produced as a companion piece to the "Missing" materials shown and discussed in Chapter One. Together they form an extended unit on crime aimed at intermediate and high intermediate students. Like "Missing," these materials were developed by Czesia Kolak, Ania Franczak, and myself. Like those materials, they focus more on receptive skills, and are a little thin on language and post-viewing activities.

The materials revolve around a one-and-a-half-minute clip from a regular Polish news broadcast that was recorded from SCOLA, the foreign-language satellite program available in the United States (see Appendix I for more details about this resource). The clip contained a news item about a violent crime committed at a local train station. As well as the face of the newscaster, it featured footage of the crime scene and the police hunt for the culprit, as well as a short comment from the suspect in his cell.

Note how the activities In these materials focus on only one section of the text at a time, so learners are not overwhelmed—in this instance the video clip as a whole would be quite wordy. Also, notice that we have devised different activities depending on the listener's needs during each section.

**Using Video: Sample Materials—Example 1: Incident at the Train Station**

# HISTORIA ZBIGNIEWA M.

## ☞ PRZED OGLĄDANIEM

- Kto i w jakiej sytuacji mógł powiedzieć te słowa:

    *"Wiedziałem, że przyjdą po mnie.*

    *Wiedziałem, że nie mam ucieczki".*

- Jakie znasz słowa, zwroty i wyrażenia typowe dla reportaży i filmów kryminalnych?

## ⌨ OGLĄDANIE REPORTAŻU TELEWIZYJNEG O

- Oglądnij reportaż bez głosu i zdecyduj jakie przestępstwo zostało popełnione.
    - ❏ włamanie
    - ❏ rabunek
    - ❏ morderstwo
    - ❏ porwanie
    - ❏ napad z bronią w ręku
    - ❏ gwałt

- Oglądnij reportaż bez wyłączania głosu. Czy twoje przypuszczenia sprawdziły się?

- Zaznacz, które z poniższych zdań są prawdziwe - P, a które fałszywe - F.

|   |   | P | F |
|---|---|---|---|
| 1. | Morderca ma 21 lat. | ____ | ____ |
| 2. | To było jego pierwsze przestępstwo. | ____ | ____ |
| 3. | Ofiarą była kasjerka. | ____ | ____ |
| 4. | Morderca czekał na policję w domu. | ____ | ____ |
| 5. | Mordercę zidentyfikował mężczyzna. | ____ | ____ |
| 6. | Morderca zdobył broń od brata. | ____ | ____ |

## ☺ ĆWICZENIA JĘZYKOWE

- Oglądnij reportaż jeszcze raz i ponumeruj zdania według kolejności ich występowania w reportażu.

    ____ Chciał wyjechać i szukać pracy na Wybrzeżu.

    ____ Zabójcą okazał się młody mężczyzna.

___ Przestępca nie stawiał oporu.

___ Podczas przesłuchania przyznał się do winy.

___ W lutym, po dwóch latach, wyszedł z więzienia.

___ Uzbrojony był w pistolet typu Mauser.

• Uzupełnij brakujące czasowniki.

Zbigniew M _____ obrabować kasę dworcową. Kiedy kasjerka zaczęła wzywać pomocy, przestępca _____ z pistoletu. Koleżanka kasjerki _____, zaalarmowana krzykiem. Udało jej się _____ _____, ponieważ morderca nie miał już naboju w pistolecie. Wówczas morderca _____ w kierunku lasu. Po 28 godzinach pościgu policja _____ _____ mordercę w jego własnym domu.

## ✎ PISANIE

• Piszemy opowiadanie kryminalne. Wszyscy uzgadniamy pierwsze zdanie, rozpoczynające opowiadanie. Zapisujemy je na kartce papieru. Pierwszy student/ka dopisuje następne zdanie i podaje kartkę dalej. Ostatni student/ka przeczyta głośno opowiadanie.

• Napisz opowiadanie kryminalne używając słów i zwrotów podanych poniżej.

| | |
|---|---|
| podejrzany/a | zastrzelić |
| morderca | uciec |
| przestępca | zbiec |
| pistolet | przyznać się do winy |
| przesłuchanie | obrabować |

## 🗣🦻 ROZMOWA

• Czy przemoc pokazywana w programach telewizyjnych może mieć negatywny wpływ na młodzież?

• Przygotować w grupach czteroosobowych *"Sąd nad Zbigniewem M ."*. Uwzględnić następujące scenki:

1. Jesteś prokuratorem. Oskarżasz Zbigniewa M.

2. Jesteś obrońcą Zbigniewa M.

3. Jesteś przewodniczącym ławy przysięgłych. Uzasadnij wyrok.

4. Jesteś sędzią. Ogłoś wyrok.

# THE STORY OF ZBIGNIEW M.

## BEFORE VIEWING

- Who might have said the following, and in what situation?:

    *"Wiedziałem, że przyjdą po mnie.*

    *Wiedziałem, że nie mam ucieczki."*

    *[I knew they would come for me.*

    *I knew I had no escape.]*

- What words and phrases do you know that are typical for crime reports and crime movies?

## WATCHING THE NEWS REPORT

- Watch the segment with the sound off and decide what type of crime was committed. Check off all that are appropriate:

    ❏ break-in

    ❏ robbery

    ❏ murder

    ❏ kidnapping

    ❏ assault with a deadly weapon

    ❏ rape

- Watch the segment again with the sound on. Were your predictions correct?

- Mark the following statements true or false, according to the story:

|  | P | F |
|---|---|---|
| 1. The murderer is 21 years old. | _____ | _____ |
| 2. This was his first offense. | _____ | _____ |
| 3. The victim was a cashier. | _____ | _____ |
| 4. The murderer waited at home for the police. | _____ | _____ |
| 5. The murderer was identified by a man. | _____ | _____ |
| 6. The murderer got the gun from his brother. | _____ | _____ |

## LANGUAGE EXERCISES

- Watch the report again and number the following sentences in the order in which they appear:

    ____ Chciał wyjechać i szukać pracy na Wybrzeżu.

    ____ Zabójcą okazał się młody mężczyzna.

___ Przestępca nie stawiał oporu.

___ Podczas przesłuchania przyznał się do winy.

___ W lutym, po dwóch latach, wyszedł z więzienia.

___ Uzbrojony był w pistolet typu Mauser.

• Fill in the missing verbs in the extract below:

Zbigniew M _____ obrabować kasę dworcową. Kiedy kasjerka zaczęła wzywać pomocy, przestępca _____ z pistoletu. Koleżanka kasjerki _____, zaalarmowana krzykiem. Udało jej się _____ _____, ponieważ morderca nie miał już naboju w pistolecie. Wówczas morderca _____ w kierunku lasu. Po 28 godzinach pościgu policja _____ _____ mordercę w jego własnym domu.

**WRITING**

• Let's write a crime story. Together we agree on the first sentence, and write it at the top of a sheet of paper. Each student writes the next sentence then passes it to his or her neighbor, and so on. The last student reads the story aloud.

• Write a crime story using the words and phrases given below.

| | |
|---|---|
| suspect | shoot |
| murderer | run away |
| criminal | get away |
| gun | confess |
| interrogation | rob |

**SPEAKING**

• Can television violence have a negative influence on young people?

• In groups of four, prepare the trial of Zbigniew M. Include the following roles and components:

1. You are the prosecutor. You bring the charges.
2. You are Zbigniew M.'s defense lawyer.
3. You are the chairperson of the jury. Explain your verdict.
4. You are the judge. Decide on the sentence.

### Example 2: Uzbek Greetings (Uzbek, beginners)

These materials were designed by Nigora Azimova of Indiana University, and use authentic video that was shot in Uzbekistan for teaching purposes. The materials, aimed at beginning students, appear in the first-year Uzbek language coursebook published by the Center for Languages of the Central Asian Region (CeLCAR) at Indiana University. The materials included here are based on three short video clips. In the first, two young women ask a young man for directions. In the second, three people introduce one another. In the last, guests are greeted at a private house. In the first and third clips, we learn a great deal of additional information about Uzbek culture: how people dress, their gestures, and the appearance of houses and streets. Note too how these materials involve the same kinds of tasks and activities we have seen elsewhere in this book.

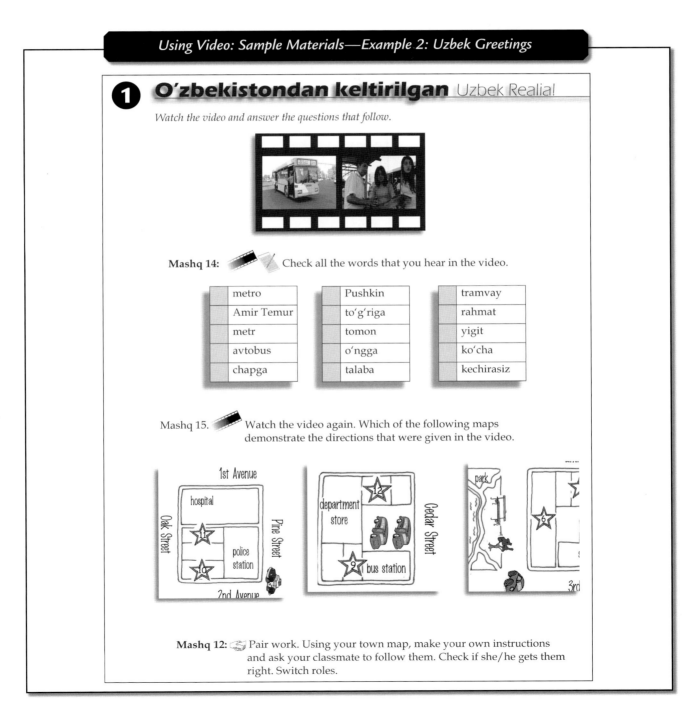

# ❷ O'zbekistondan keltirilgan Uzbek Realia!

*Watch the video once and check the box with the correct answer.*

Mashq 11. What are the names of the people in the video?

| 1. girl with her hair down | | 2. girl with ponytail | | 3. guy | |
|---|---|---|---|---|---|
| Laylo | | Malika | | Dilshod | |
| Farida | | Farida | | Akmal | |
| Zebiniso | | Laylo | | Farruh | |

**Mashq 12:** Watch the video one more time and find out where the people are from.

_____

_____

_____

**Mashq 13:** Now watch the video for the last time and fill in the blanks with the information you have already learned from the video.

Assalomu alaykum, qalaysizlar? _____?
Rahmat, o'zingiz yaxshimisiz?
Sizlar _____?
Men _____?
Men ham
Voy, qanday yaxshi!
Men ham _____, lekin men Samarqanddanman.
Otim _____, sizniki-chi?
Meniki _____
Tanishganimdan xursandman

_____

Men ham, juda ham

*What is the other word for "mening"?* _____
*Did you notice how people pronounce the word "men", how?* _____
*What is the other word for 'ism'- name?* _____

# ❸ O'zbekistondan keltirilgan Uzbek Realia!

In this part of the lesson we will learn ...

**Mashq 8:** Watch the video without any sound and note the non-verbal behavior of the participants.

| SPEAKERS | ACTIONS |
|---|---|
| Man with traditional hat and man with necktie on | |
| Man with traditional hat and man with furry hat | |
| Woman and man | |
| Women together | |

**Mashq 9:** Now watch with sound once again as they greet and match the expressions on the left with the responses on the right.

| | EXPRESSIONS | | RESPONSE |
|---|---|---|---|
| 1 | Assalomu alaykum. | | Xudoga shukur. |
| 2 | Yaxshimisiz? | | Yaxshi, rahmat. |
| 3 | Bolalar yaxshimi? | | Vaalaykum assalom |

**Mashq 10:** With a partner, create a short dialogue and then act it out.

## Example 3: Vinci (Polish, intermediate)

This example is part of a unit on the Polish city of Kraków. It revolves around *Vinci,* a 2004 comedy thriller by Juliusz Machulski about a plan to steal Leonardo da Vinci's "Lady with an Ermine," the most famous painting in Poland, which hangs in Kraków's Czartoryski Museum. The point of entry for this set of exercises is a line from the film: "There's only one painting in Poland" (*"Jest tylko jeden obraz w Polsce"*). The activities shown here concentrate on listening using short extracts from two key scenes in the film. In the first scene Cuma, a professional thief, tries to interest his former partner Julian, who is now a cop, in taking part in the robbery of the painting. In the second, Julian asks Magda, a talented art student, how much she could charge for a forgery of the painting.

---

### Using Video: Sample Materials—Example 3: Vinci

**Level:**

Intermediate/Upper Intermediate

**Pre-viewing**

"Jest tylko jeden obraz w Polsce." (*"There's only one picture in Poland."*)

Which picture is the speaker referring to? Why does he say this?

*Film still courtesy of Juliusz Machulski*

**Viewing Activity 1**

1. Watch the clip. Wave your hand when you hear the sentence above.
2. Watch the clip again and put the parts of the dialogue in order:

Number in sequence:

a. Da Vinci?                                         _____

b. Dlaczego? Za milion euro? Można.         _____

c. Za to nie piję.                                     _____

d. Co, za ostre?                                      _____

e. No, to za Vinci!                                   _____

f. W Polsce jest tylko jeden obraz.           _____

g. Skąd wiesz?                                        _____

h. Obraz, co ci mówiłem, wisi u Czartoryskich.      __1__

**Viewing Activity 2**

1. Before viewing the second clip, read through the parts of the dialogue. Arrange them into the sequence that seems most natural.

*Film still courtesy of Juliusz Machulski*

Dobra, a ile czasu potrzebujesz? *(Fine; how much time do you need?)*

Koszty plus milion. *(Costs plus a million.)*

Dwa miesiące. *(Two months.)*

Zaraz, zaraz! Jakie gites? A cena? *(Wait a minute. What do you mean, cool? What about the price?)*

Moment. Mówimy tu o 200 tysiącach euro? Za jeden obrazek??? *(Just a minute. We're talking about 200 thousand euros? For one picture?)*

Okej. *(OK.)*

A ile mam? *(How much do I have?)*

Okej, to gites! *(OK, cool!)*

Zajebiście pracochłonny obrazek! To jest trudniejsze do malowania niż oryginał! *(A hell of a time-consuming picture! It's harder to paint than the original!)*

Stary milion to zapłacisz za mnie za kawę. Milion polskich nowych złotych. *(An old million is what my coffee'll cost. A million new Polish zlotys.)*

No, mów! *(You name it!)*

Co? co? To znaczy co? Stary milion? *(What was that? What do you mean? An old million?)*

2. Watch the second clip and see if you are right.

3. Who is the woman in this scene? What do you think is going on?

## Extensive Viewing

As suggested above, extensive viewing of video is not as linguistically useful as intensive viewing. Nevertheless, if used in combination, it can be an interesting supplement to intensive work, which can be very demanding. Tasks can also be designed around extensive viewing. Be careful, though, not to make these tasks dependent on the kind of detailed listening that intensive tasks require. For example, "What did X say in such-and-such a scene?" is not a good kind of question for an extensive listening activity. Rather, focus on broad issues: plot, characters, relationships, settings, costumes, and action. For example:

### Characters

Choose an interesting character from the film. Describe her. What does she look like? What are some of her personality traits? What are her goals? What happened to this character before the movie begins? What will happen to her after it ends?

### Plot

What do you think are the key turning points in the plot? How else might the story have developed at these moments? If you were writing the film, what changes would you make in the storyline?

### Costumes

Choose one of the characters. How does he dress? What colors and kinds of clothes does he wear? What does this say about him as a person?

Many of the activities suggested in Bamford and Day's book on extensive reading can be adapted for use with extensive viewing tasks (see the Resources section of Chapter Two).

## Resources

The following books give more ideas for creative and effective ways of using video in the language classroom.

Cooper, R., Lavery, M., & Rinvolucri, M. (1991). *Video*. Oxford: Oxford University Press.

Lonergan, J. (1984). *Video in language teaching*. Cambridge: Cambridge University Press.

Sherman, J. (2003). *Using authentic video in the language classroom*. Cambridge: Cambridge University Press.

Stempleski, S., & Arcario, P. (Eds.). (1992). *Video in language teaching: Using, selecting, and producing video for the classroom*. Alexandria, VA: TESOL.

Stempleski, S., & Tomalin, B. (1990). *Video in action: Recipes for using video in language teaching*. New York: Prentice Hall.

# Chapter Five
# Visual Materials: Using Pictures

## Introduction

When I was about ten years old, I began French classes at school. The teacher mostly relied on large board-mounted pictures, such as a street scene or department store, which she would hold up for the class to see. Our job was to describe in French the objects and activities in the picture: "There is a truck at the corner," "The old woman is buying bread," and so on. Even all these years later, I can still remember how satisfying it was to make a connection between the new language and things and actions I could see.

Many teachers use pictures the way my French teacher did to encourage students, especially at lower levels, to use the language they have been taught to describe (images of) real-world phenomena. On the second day of a Pashto class I recently attended, the teacher did just this, showing us pictures of Afghans and asking us: "Is this a young girl?" "Is this an old man?" and so on. The connection between language and visual images helps us to move beyond a reliance on translation and to associate words directly with the objects and actions they relate to. As learners acquire greater competence in the language, they can be challenged to be more productive in using the target language to describe a person, landscape, or interior scene that they are shown in a picture.

There's nothing harmful about such activities, and many learners enjoy them in moderation. Yet it's also true that the kind of activities I've just described are somewhat mechanistic, and may even seem meaningless—why would we want to describe something to someone else when that other person can already see the picture? When considered in this light, such activities seem little more than another variant of the "display of knowledge" that characterizes many classrooms yet involves little or no real communication.

For me, the real joy of pictures lies in the fact that, while they can stimulate an active response of the kind seen with written and filmed texts, they typically contain little or no language, and so are capable of encouraging correspondingly rich language from the students. In other words, unconstrained by language in the input, learners produce even richer language in the output when responding to the pictures. In this section, then, the activities suggested go beyond describing what is in the picture; the emphasis will be on stimulating learners' creativity and imagination with the use of images, and on tapping personal responses to these images.

Just as earlier I used the word "video" as shorthand for any recorded moving images so here I'll use "picture" to mean anything from a photograph to a painting. Where one particular kind of picture is meant I will specify.

Though numerous books on teaching offer ideas for using pictures, the best source devoted exclusively to such activities is *The Mind's Eye,* by Alan Maley, Alan Duff, and Françoise Grellet (see the Resources at the end of this chapter for publication details). The ideas presented in this chapter are meant only to give a flavor of the possibilities that exist; the selection is based primarily on what I have found to be especially effective in stimulating student talking and listening. Since pictures involve little or no language input work, and constitute as it were their own point of entry, I have listed just a few different kinds of activities that can involve pictures. Any of these can be integrated with other materials described elsewhere in this book, and in fact I recommend strongly that you think about doing so—many of these activities would make excellent pre-reading, pre-viewing, or pre-listening activities when combined thematically with interesting written or spoken texts. Also, when suggesting these activities I am thinking primarily of their use in classroom speaking activities, with the students in pairs or small groups; but the kinds of questions I suggest could also be used as a starting point for written activities.

## My Father Falls Off a Mountain

Always a minimalist, I've learned that the students themselves provide the best material for language learning activities. In this case this is literally true. In my wallet I keep a picture of my father. I show the class this photo and tell them the story of the day my father fell off a mountain during a hike we took together, when I had to go and summon the mountain rescue team. I then ask if anyone else has a personal photograph in their wallet or purse. There is always at least one person in three (nearly always more) who has such a picture. I ask the learners to get into pairs or small groups, to talk about the person or people in the pictures and to tell a story about an experience they had together. This is a very nice warm-up activity for the first few minutes of class, and serves the additional purpose of helping the learners to get to know one another.

### *People and Places*

When using pictures of people and of places, you don't have to restrict your activities to describing them. A more interactive approach is to ask the students to speculate upon, or engage with, the image. For example, study the following picture of a man:

*Photo courtesy of Kasia Rydel-Johnston*

After asking students to describe what they see, we might follow up with some questions such as:

- Who do you think this person is?

- Is he wealthy?

- Is he happy?

- What's his job?

- What is he holding in his hand?

- What is he doing with this object?

- Where was this picture taken?

Likewise, when using a picture of a place, we can initially ask students merely to describe it to make sure they have the basic vocabulary, but then we can go further. With the following picture, we might ask:

- Whose room is this?

- What can you tell about this person from their room?

- What activities go on in this room?

- Why is it decorated this way?

- If it were your room, how would you decorate it differently?

- What can be seen from the windows?

*Photo courtesy of the LCTL Project at CARLA*

## Being Part of the Picture

It's sometimes said that we need language in order to be able to describe the world around us. This is certainly true. It is this purpose for language learning that my French teacher drew on in asking us to describe what we saw in the street scene. But I often think that in our language learning we are overly concerned with this connection between language and the world. Language also serves another function, at least as important—that of allowing us to express our imagination and creativity: to imagine non-existent worlds, to speculate on what might have been, and to put ourselves in others' shoes. Many of the activities in this chapter promote this other, creative and imaginative use of language rather than the more down-to-earth use that is emphasized elsewhere.

Here's an example of what I mean. Take a look at the picture below:

*Photo courtesy of the LCTL Project at CARLA*

Imagine you are one of the people in the picture (you can choose which one).

- Who are you?

- What is your relationship with the other people in the picture?

- Who took the picture?

- Where was the picture taken?

- What was the occasion?

- What were you doing before the picture was taken?

- What did you do after the picture was taken?

- Who else has a copy of this picture?

(Add more questions if you like!)

## *Who Took the Photograph?*

Contemporary art criticism has reminded us that a picture-—a photograph, say—doesn't just exist in a vacuum. Someone took the picture; they took it for a reason; they chose to take this picture and not another, and to include some things and not others. This is particularly true of photographs taken by professional photographers for magazines and newspapers.

These issues can be the starting point for very creative activities in the language classroom, in part because they not only encourage the use of new, genuinely creative and communicative language, but also because they teach students to think about the world differently. As Neil Postman has observed, part of the problem with the switch from words to images I mentioned in Chapter Four is that, unlike words, pictures cannot be said to be right or wrong—they just "are." One can disagree with things expressed in language, challenging their truthfulness for example; but it's a lot harder to disagree with a picture. Yet, just as with the analysis of television news suggested in the previous chapter, pictures too can be seen to take sides and carry values. Once one begins to think about such things, it often permanently changes the way one looks at published pictures.

Below is one example of using a photograph in this way. Take a look at the following picture.

*Photo courtesy of the LCTL Project at CARLA*

In pairs, discuss the following questions:

- Who took this picture?

- When was it taken and where?

- Why was the picture taken?

- Who was it taken for?

- What is excluded from the picture—what appears outside the frame?

- What effect might this picture have on those seeing it, for example in a newspaper?

- If you were the photographer, how might you change the way this picture was taken?

## Mystery Pictures

Some pictures are more mysterious than others; we can't quite figure out what they're showing or what they mean. Yet this immediately piques our curiosity and leads us to speculate. Such kinds of pictures are great for stimulating language use. For example, look at the following picture:

*Photo courtesy of Kasia Rydel-Johnston*

You might give your students the following task: In groups of three, decide on an interpretation of this picture. When you have finished, present your interpretation to the rest of the class. Which group came up with the most convincing account?

## Every Picture Tells a Story

One of the most powerful human impulses is the need to tell stories and to make narratives. Many pictures can be used to exploit this impulse. Look at the following picture, and consider these questions:

- What is happening in this picture?

- What is everyone watching?

- What events led up to the point at which the picture was taken?

- What happened afterwards?

- Who was involved and how are they related to one another?

The urge to tell stories is particularly noticeable when we are faced with a group of three or four apparently disparate pictures; our natural tendency is to find some way of linking them, since we like things to be related rather than disconnected.

Take a look at the following four pictures.

These four pictures tell a story. In what order were they taken? How are they linked? What story do they tell?

These may seem simple questions, but agreeing on a story, writing it, and reading it to the other students is a great group activity that can usefully occupy the students for a considerable stretch of time, and can force them to draw on all their language resources in telling their story.

## *Entering the Picture*

Other pictures seem to invite us to enter them. Look at the following picture:

Many activities are possible with this kind of picture. For example:

1.  Imagine you witnessed this fire. Describe the scene from your point of view, as if you were writing a journal.

2.  Write a dialogue between two of the people involved in this story.

3.  You are a newspaper reporter. Write a report of the incident shown in the picture.

4.  Write a poem about the incident shown in the picture.

5.  Imagine you are a newspaper editor. What would be the headline of the story in which this picture appears? What caption would you write for the picture itself?

## *Family Photo Album*

As the opening activity in this section suggests, pictures with a personal meaning are great for encouraging students to talk and listen. Many different activities are possible with family photos. Here are a few ideas:

1.  Ask each student to bring in a picture of her- or himself as a small child. Mix the photos up on the desk at the front. Have the students gather round and guess which picture shows which student. This will naturally lead to a lot of talk about facial features, how people have changed, resemblances and so on—all good language learning material.

2.  Ask students to bring a family picture, and have them talk to their colleagues in groups about the members of their family shown in the picture.

3.  Have students bring in a picture of an older relative; ask them to use the picture as a starting-point for describing that person's physical appearance and character, and for describing their own relationship with this relative.

4. Ask students to each bring a picture from a family occasion that held meaning for them. Again in groups, have them describe the occasion—what happened and why it was important to them.

5. Ask students to bring in a picture of a close relative. In groups, the other students have to look at the picture, guess who the relative is, and find out as much about him or her as they can, but only by asking the owner of the picture yes-no questions.

## In the Art Gallery

Paintings can also be a good source of images to use in class. "Modern" art in particular is often suitable—the abstract or surreal images stimulate the imagination and offer an easier route to a discussion of different possible interpretations than is usually the case with "traditional" representational art. As with the other kinds of pictures considered in this section, the lack of language in most paintings means that the learner's own language use arises from direct contact with the content of the picture—unlike, say, with poems, in which the learner must first understand the basic meaning of the text before responding.

Many sorts of pictures can be used, and to many different purposes. The following activity is based around *The Blue Circus* by Marc Chagall. This picture is widely available in art books and on the Internet.

Take a look at the picture. In pairs, try and decide what the painting is saying. In particular, what do you think is the significance of the following elements:

- The fish
- The trapeze artist
- The horse
- The moon
- The chicken
- What is the meaning of the colors and shapes the artist chose?
- What do you make of the figure in the bottom right-hand corner?

Be creative in your interpretations!

## Strip Cartoons: Fill in the Bubbles

The following activity is much harder than it might sound—I'd recommend using it only with intermediate or advanced students.

Take a strip cartoon and cover up the language in the speech bubbles (see the following example). The learners' task is to work in pairs to fill in the bubbles with their own dialogue. The learners' language practice comes not just from the dialogue they create, but above all from the work of negotiating the story with their partner.

As a closing activity, pairs can read their dialogues aloud to the rest of the class or display them on the wall.

This activity can work either with a cartoon taken from the target culture or with one familiar from the L1 culture (in workshops, for example, I've had some brilliant Russian stories based on a "Peanuts" cartoon). The example below is from an American comic strip entitled "Welcome to Falling Rock National Park" by Josh Shalek. Cartoons of different length are possible—the kind that involve only three or four frames are obviously easier to do than the longer cartoons of perhaps 10 or 12 frames which appear in Sunday papers in the U.S.

Comic strip courtesy of Josh Shalek

## Variations:

To give the task a little more focus or to make it a bit easier, you could:

- leave the language in the first frame;

- leave the language in the last frame;

- leave the language in both first and last frames;

- provide some of the words or phrases used;

- any combination of the above.

In fact, another variant on this, for lower levels, would simply be to make this a reading task—provide them with the text of all the speech bubbles, mixed up, and ask them to figure out what goes where. This kind of task isn't very creative but does help with reading comprehension and sensitizes learners to discourse features that organize extended language use such as conversations.

## The Invisible Photograph

I hope that throughout this book, and especially in this chapter, I have demonstrated that the key ingredient for good language learning is not a perfect, ready-made set of materials, but imagination and creativity. The following activity is a perfect illustration of this point. It involves nothing but blank sheets of paper!

This activity is suitable for students of any level from lower intermediate upwards. I take a stack of blank pieces of white paper (photocopying paper is fine) and give one to each student. I then explain that what they have in front of them is a favorite personal photograph of theirs. I hold up my picture and describe it to them, telling them both what is in the picture and why it is so meaningful to me. My picture (usually) shows my younger daughter, Helen, when she was about two years old. She is sitting on a bench, her very short legs dangling above the ground, her finger characteristically in her mouth. The light comes from behind her through a slatted Venetian blind, falling on her long, fair hair and on the floor. The picture was taken during a family outing to a museum in York, England. I like it because it's a beautiful picture; but I have to admit that it gives a false picture of Helen—she looks so innocent and quiet, whereas she was a very active child—quite a handful in reality!

Helen in the Museum

I like this activity for what I think are several good reasons. It draws on the learners' imagination; it is individualized; it involves real meaning; it is personal; and it calls on effective language use— because there's no actual picture present—all meaning must be conveyed linguistically. And lastly, it almost always works! It took some courage to do the first time I tried it, but having seen many different groups of learners take to it enthusiastically, I now have the confidence to use it often.

## Resources

As mentioned above, the best source for using pictures that I know of is this book:

Maley, A., Duff, A., & Grellet, F. (1981). *The mind's eye.* Cambridge: Cambridge University Press.

Another book worth looking at is:

Bovin, M. (2000). *Every picture tells a story.* Niagara Falls, NY: Full Blast Productions.

You should also be aware of the following books, which help artistically challenged teachers such as myself to include graphic elements in their classes:

Wright, A. (1989). *Pictures for language learning.* Cambridge: Cambridge University Press.

Wright, A. (1985). *1000 pictures for teachers to copy.* London: Longman.

As far as pictures themselves are concerned, my favorite sources are high-quality color periodicals such as *National Geographic* and *Smithsonian Magazine.* Of course, copying such pictures in a textbook you publish would involve copyright issues, but as long as use is restricted to your classroom this should note pose a problem (for more on this issue, see the Appendix II on Copyright).

# Chapter Six
# Creating Integrated Skills Packets

Integrated skills packets are extensive sets of materials that revolve around a central topic or subject and include practice in multiple language skills as part of the activities designed around the texts. They typically involve at least two different sets of the kinds of materials described in previous chapters—for example, a video segment and a reading.

In this chapter we'll look at some of the main issues to consider when making an integrated skills packet, and we will see some examples of such packets.

## Why Integrated Skills Packets?

Why is there a separate chapter on integrated skills? In other words, how are integrated skills packets different from the kinds of activities we have looked at so far, designed around a single text such as a newspaper article, song, or video clip?

In some ways there's no major difference, and to an extent integrated skills packets are merely sequences of two or more such groups of activities. In these terms, the only big difference is in the scope of the activity.

There is, however, much more to the matter than this. The reason I am emphasizing integrated skills activities in a separate chapter is that they constitute what for many of the less commonly taught languages is a radically new approach to teaching the language. As mentioned in earlier chapters, language teaching has traditionally been "about" language. In this traditional kind of approach, the topics covered are things like past tense, perfective versus imperfective aspect, adjectives, and so on. Of course, learners do need to know these features of the language they are learning. Yet research has shown that learners learn better and more willingly when the language is mostly used for something beyond itself—in other words, when there is a focus on content, not form. The most extreme, but also the most effective, application of this idea is to be found in American primary and secondary education, where content-based language instruction has been found to be very successful in helping immigrant children to master English, and in language immersion programs, helping English-speaking children learn French or Spanish. Content-based teaching takes the substance of materials (perhaps history or social studies) as a starting point, and builds language work around the students' needs in reading, writing, speaking, and listening about the content. Work on grammar, for example, arises naturally from what the learners encounter in dealing with content. Such practices have yet to be widely adopted in foreign language teaching in universities and other settings (aside from some post-secondary Language Across the Curriculum classes). Yet large amounts of evidence indicate that these content-based approaches offer an excellent and extremely effective way of engaging with the language being learned.

The kinds of activities described in preceding chapters constitute one step towards a focus on content, though they only go part of the way. For many teachers who use a song or a video clip in class, these activities remain marginal—supplementary to the prime curriculum, which remains grammar-based. Integrated skills packets offer another major step away from primarily grammar-based teaching and towards a focus on using language *for* something. Such materials move us towards a direct association between the language being learned and the kinds of purposes that can be achieved by learning it.

If I were to design an entire curriculum, say for Polish, it would be composed almost exclusively of topics—concrete subjects from the real world that the learners would read, write, listen, and speak about in and through the target language. In other words, the whole thing would involve integrated skills. Much of this would come from the target culture, using authentic materials to read, watch, and listen to about issues, people, and events in today's Poland. The more advanced the learners, the more prominent this approach would become. Integrated skills packets, organized in terms of content topics, are an important step towards this kind of syllabus.

## Issues in Creating Integrated Skills Packets

As was said about materials development around individual texts (in chapters 2–5), there are no hard and fast rules about developing integrated skills packets. Each group of materials suggests its own uses. It's partly for this reason that this book as a whole has aimed more at giving suggestions for creative ways of using materials rather than laying down strict rules about how this is to be done. This is part of the nature of using authentic materials, which come in such a wide diversity of shapes and sizes. It's also part of the essence of teaching, since each teacher brings a unique set of creative ideas and energy to the job of coming up with classroom activities, and each group of learners has different interests and preferences.

But at the same time, it's worth mentioning a few guidelines and issues to be thinking about; these have emerged over the course of many years of developing these kinds of materials, and I find it helpful to bear such things in mind as I work on materials development.

### Keep It Specific

Often, when teachers think about topics in language teaching they think in terms of broad subjects like "sports," "politics," "health." Once such a general subject is raised, one's first instinct is to begin by giving the learners all the most important vocabulary for that topic. This is a mistake! Though the learners may "have" the vocabulary in the sense that it's written down in their notebooks, they're unlikely to remember much of it because it's not attached to anything meaningful or concrete. The vocabulary they learn from content-focused lessons will be less thorough, but they'll retain it much better because they encounter it in context, attached to specific meanings. This has been found to be true in numerous studies of vocabulary learning and reading.

It's much better to have a narrower, more specific topic. "Sports" is not a good topic; "Super Bowl 2007" is. "Politics" is not a good topic; "The Polish elections of 2005" is. "Health" isn't good; an episode of *ER* is. Each of these topics will contain only a fragment of the total vocabulary for the broader subject they form a part of; but they will be infinitely more engaging than a generalized topic that ends up being about nothing in particular, and the learners will learn vastly more in terms of the grammar, sociolinguistic rules, and other aspects of language that apply to this topic in the target language.

## *Topic Selection is a Dialogue*

As I have said already about many aspects of materials development, the selection of topics is a dialogical process: you need to think about your own interests and knowledge, but also the interests of the students. It's crucial—and strangely liberating—to continually ask oneself: What most interests my particular students? A case in point is music. The older I get, the more my musical tastes diverge from those of my students. Yet I've found that when it comes to working with songs in class, it's best to ask the students what they like listening to, and to work with that, rather than impose my own (admittedly rather idiosyncratic) preferences. Likewise, when using video in ESL classes it's good to begin by asking my students what TV programs they enjoy watching and would like to work with. This has sometimes led me to use materials I would not normally choose—a couple of years ago, by popular student request we worked on an episode of *The Jerry Springer Show*—but I feel that this is all for the best. As well as motivating the students, it's a learning experience for me too.

In second language contexts like ESL in the United States it's possible to give students these kinds of opportunities for input. But in foreign language teaching, the students are unlikely to be familiar with the popular or other cultures of the language being studied. This is where the dialogue comes in. As someone who does know the target culture or cultures, the teacher can introduce the students to readings, listenings, and viewings that they will find interesting. This process has two distinct aspects. One involves material that is culturally highly important and is good for students to know. Any student of Polish needs to know about Adam Mickiewicz, the national poet; about Chopin; about the 19th Century uprisings, the Second World War and the Holocaust, and the communist period, including the Solidarity opposition. This kind of knowledge is the teacher's contribution to the dialogue mentioned earlier—these are things that the students are unlikely to come up with on their own, since they may know little or nothing about them, or may initially think them uninteresting.

But another way in which the teacher can contribute to the dialogue is to see the target culture through the eyes of the students, rather than those of a teacher. Take the case of Poland and Polish culture. Any student of Polish culture should know something about the great poets and writers, the painters and composers, and about Poland's dramatic and fascinating history, and certainly these things should be part of their education. But the Poland of the early 21st century is a very different kind of place than that represented by much of the Polish cultural tradition. Since 1989 the country has been a free and independent capitalist democracy. There is a whole generation—anyone under the age of 30 or so—for whom the communist era and the political struggle of Solidarity is a distant childhood memory. Today's young Poles use cell phones and internet cafes, go on vacation in foreign countries, and watch MTV. Their passports allow them to travel freely in Europe and elsewhere. The country as a whole faces an entirely new set of problems—unemployment, political corruption, the erosion of women's rights, and the controversial role of the Catholic church.

In thinking about what topics I might include in a Polish course, I ask myself what my students would find interesting. Polish rap music, SMS etiquette, problems of drug use and violence in schools—these things are rather remote from my own experiences, but are much closer to those of young American university students than Solidarity or the wartime years. This is where one can also search for ideas for topics. When I'm in Poland, I look around and see what young people are doing. What movies are they going to? What magazines do they read? What are the most popular Polish bands? What organizations do young people belong to? How do they spend their free time? These questions provide a starting point for the search for materials that will be culturally appropriate, but will speak to U.S. university students in the most direct way possible.

## Matching Materials

It's usually quite difficult to find materials on a given topic that match each other perfectly. Authentic materials being what they are—designed for purposes other than language pedagogy—are rarely neatly integrated with one another. We just have to accept this, and work with pairs or sets of texts that are somewhat disparate. In fact, it's more important that the texts should be interesting in themselves, and should allow for recycling of important language (see below), than that they should be ideally complementary.

## Sequencing

As was mentioned in the chapter on listening, the sequencing of activities is as important as the activities themselves. Activities should build on one another; each one should enable subsequent ones. They should grow progressively in complexity, in length, and in difficulty.

## Recycling Language

One of the greatest advantages of integrated skills materials is that they give learners the opportunity to recycle receptive and productive vocabulary, grammar, and other aspects of language. This kind of recycling is known to be extremely important in learning new language. In designing integrated skills materials it's crucial to deliberately incorporate such recycling into the activities.

Typically, this comes from multiple opportunities to engage with words, phrases, bits of grammar and so on that are associated with the topic in question. Again typically, this language is first encountered receptively through reading, listening, or viewing; subsequently the learners have a chance to use the new language themselves through writing and speaking activities. As concerns the first step, it's extremely advantageous for learners to encounter a new word, phrase, or grammatical structure not just in one text, but in two different texts; this will be of considerable help in the process of learning the new linguistic material.

In designing activities for the learners, it's vital to find tasks that will oblige them to re-use some of the language they've encountered in the texts they've been reading or listening to. Some examples of these kinds of tasks can be seen below.

We will now take a look at three different integrated skills packets. For each example I've made some comments underlining how the above principles have been followed in the design of the activities.

# Examples of Integrated Skills Packets

### Example 1: When Bear was Hungry (Ojibwe, lower intermediate)

These Ojibwe-language materials were prepared by Elyse Carter Vosen of the College of St. Scholastica. The materials draw on two related texts about berry-picking. The first is an audio recording of a story told by Earl Nyholm, originally published in *Oshkaabewis Native Journal, Vol. 2, No.1* (Fall 1995), entitled "When Bear Was Hungry." Elyse Carter Vosen's translation of the tale is presented below. The second text comprises scenes from a television documentary about Ojibwe elder couple Dorothy and Darwin Stevens of the White Earth Reservation in Minnesota, in which the couple pick chokecherries. Elyse has developed a series of interactive activities around these two texts—note how she incorporates the ideas, reactions, and experiences of the learners in the course of the unit, which nevertheless is centered on traditional Ojibwe cultural practices.

## Integrated Skills Packets—Example 1: When Bear Was Hungry

**Context for this Unit:**

· Designed for use toward the very end of a college/university second semester Beginning Ojibwemowin course.

· "Makwa Bekaded" would be used over the course of two class periods, and "Mawinzowin" for two class periods.

**Objectives:**

· Observe and analyze humor, especially in terms of imagery and gesture inherent in the language.

· Demonstrate listening comprehension. Recognize and understand B-form sentence constructions.

· Describe extended family relationships, especially relationships between grandmothers and grandchildren in Ojibwemowin.

· Be able to identify and locate several types of berries for picking.

· Recognize special storytelling inflections, pitches, gestures, exclamations, and a fluent speaker's use of emphatics.

## MAKWA BEKADED *(WHEN BEAR WAS HUNGRY)*

jibwaa-pizindaawin *(before you listen)*

Makwa bekaded? Ginisidotaan ina? *(The bear is hungry? Do you understand it?)*

Wegonen waasiniwaad, makwag? *(What do bears eat?)*

Take a BLANK PHOTOGRAPH and work in pairs. Think about a bear...describe this picture you've taken of a bear doing something.

Ningii-atoonan niizh oshki-ikidowinan omaa:

(I've put two new words here that you need):

**bawa'iminagaawanzh na** pincherry bush

**bawa'iminaan ni** pincherry

inaashke: other berry plants and their berries (miinagaawanzh/miin) often have the same relationship (animate/inanimate)

Bizindan dibaajimowin. Listen especially for emphatics (go, igo, sa) and for exclamations (Howah! Tayaa! Hai!). Write your favorite when you hear it.

### When Bear Was Hungry

Told by Earl Nyholm; translated by Elyse Carter Vosen

(1) A long, long time ago, there was a certain thing that happened. (2) One time Bear went home looking hungry. (3) And while he was walking around, trying to look for something he could eat, he saw a lot of pincherries hanging low there on a pincherry bush. (4) And then when he began to climb up there, into that tree, in vain he did it, and even harder he tried in vain to grab hold of those pincherries. (5) Well then, that was it, further and further into the sky there he climbed, always without result. (6) Well, darn it! (7) And there it was, that Bear could not get a taste of even one pincherry. (8) Well then, so it was that he went down from the tree in a certain way, and now he got ready to leave. (9) And as he left, and was on his way home that he said, "There's one thing for certain! They sure aren't very strong, those pincherry trees!"

ishkwaa-pizindawin

bezhig:

Look at the Ojibwe text and imagine the gestures of Earl Nyholm as he tells the story. The second time we listen, act them out.

niizh:

Aandi gaa-izhaad, Makwa? Waawiyebii'igen i'iw mazinaakizon.

niswi:

Daga ozhibii'igen "X" omaa.

|  | EYA | GAAWIIN |
|---|---|---|
| Gii-akwaandawe na, Makwa? |  |  |
| Gii-wiisin ina? |  |  |
| Gii-minwendam ina? |  |  |
| Gii-nishkaadizi na? |  |  |
| Gii-maajaa na? |  |  |

niiwin:

Shrink the story into a three-line makwa poem. Ozhibii'igen omaa.

niiwiin:

Bakadeyaan, aaniin daa-izhichigeyan?

MAWINZOWIN

Nookomisag & Noozisag

Two scenes from *Mino-Bimaadiziwin: The Good Life*

*The film follows Dorothy and Darwin Stevens, an elder couple from White Earth reservation, along with other members of the community, through a cycle of seasonal cultural practices/ceremonies. The film illustrates the importance of gathering to the traditional economy and to the concept of mimo-bimaadiziwin.*

jibwaa-waabiwin:

Gimawinz ina? Awenen wiiji-mawinzoyan? *(Do you go berry picking? Who do you pick berries with?)*

Aaniin gaa-aabajitooyan? *(How do you use them?)* Talk to a partner and explain, using Ojibwemowin and gestures.

bezhig:

Ganawaabandan dibaajimowin mazinaate-makakong. *(Watch the video.)*

Awenenag ayaawag omaa? Aaniin enawendiwag? *(Who is there? How are they related?)* Make a list of people with your partner.

SCENE BEZHIG:

Dorothy and Darwin are picking chokecherries in the late afternoon by the shore of a lake. The wind blowing the branches can be heard, and there are close shots of the berries, which are red and vibrant. The camera focuses first on Darwin, who is picking quietly with a smile on his face, and then on Dorothy. She comments, "We don't need too many...not too much, eh?" She puts a few cherries in her mouth.

SCENE NIIZH:

Dorothy's kitchen is filled with steam. Kettles boil on the stove. There are shots of her calendar, pictures of her grandchildren. Dorothy and her daughter sit together talking at the table. Three grandchildren, aged about two, four, and six, are happily jumping on her bed. "I hope it turns out to be jelly. Or at least I hope it turns out to be edible." She and her daughter laugh.

niizh:

Put the events below in order according to when they happen in the video:

_____ Gwashkwaaniwag nibaaganing, abinoojiyensag.

_____ Zhoomiingweni, akiwenzii. Ogojipidaanan i'iw asasaweminan, mindemoye.

_____ Adoopowining wiiji-giigidowag idash wiiji-baapiwag, mindemoye gaye ginaanis.

_____ Zaaga'iganing mawinzowag, mindemoye, akiwenzii gaye.

Why are these two scenes put together in the film?

Aaniin menwendaman? Aaniin wenaanimiziyan? *(What makes you happy? In what way are you confused?)*

niswi:

Ganoozh gikinoo'amaagan. Mikanan ikidowinan ji atooyan akina makakong omaa.

| | IZHINIKAADEWIN/ IZHINIKAAZOWIN *(HOW IT IS NAMED)* | GIIZIS ATITEMAGAK/ ATISOD *(THE MONTH IT IS RIPE)* | AYAAWIN MIKIGAADED/ MIKIGAAZOD *(WHERE IT IS FOUND)* |
|---|---|---|---|
| | miskomin *(raspberry)* | ishpi-aabita-giizis *(in the middle of the month)* | gitigaaning, zagaateg *(in planted ground)* |
| | | | |

niiwin:

Gakina gegoo Dorothy ogikinoo'amawaag noozisag. *(Dorothy teachers her grandchildren many things.)*

Wegonen gekinawaabiyan gikinoo'amaaged, Gookomis? *(What do you learn when your Grandma teaches?)*

Create a short story, a poem, or a song about your Grandma.

### Example 2: The Sami (Norwegian, beginning to advanced)

These Norwegian language materials, aimed at high school students of varying language abilities, were designed by Valerie Borey of Concordia Language Villages. The materials concern the Sami or Lapps, an ethnic group living in the far north of the Scandinavian countries. In these materials, note the wide range of kinds of materials and activities included, and also the way these activities are designed to involve mixed-ability groups.

---

**Integrated Skills Packets—Example 2: The Sami**

**Target Audience:**

High-school students, with abilities ranging from beginning to advanced

**Setting:**

Norwegian immersion program humanities class (high-school credit received)

**Objectives:**

- Introduce contemporary Sami figures and contrast them with more traditional depictions
- Engage a variety of learning strategies/interests through independent, social, artistic, and analytical means
- Arouse the interest of younger villagers in non-credit program
- Revitalize Skogfjorden's current collection of Sami props

**Day One**

Step 1: Twenty-five students of various language abilities are divided into five groups, each group representing a range of ability (low-high).

Step 2: Each group is given one of five short illustrated articles to read aloud. Questions are answered as a group.

Step 3: Students receive paints (colors labeled) and a plywood board with a face-shaped hole cut in the center. Their objective is to paint a picture that best represents the person(s) in the article and his/her/their setting—but not to duplicate the photograph in the article.

Step 4: Reading assignment from Sami textbook (in English). Written reflection (1 page in English due the following day): *What are the differences between how Sami are represented in the textbook and how they are represented in the article you read? What are the similarities?*

**Day Two**

Step 5: Discuss reflections, touch on the role of nature, time-frame, and visual imagery.

Step 6: Groups do the final touches on their paintings.

Step 7: Once paintings are set out to dry, each group must come up with 5 key words (clues) that best illustrate the article they read. These should be written on slips of paper (one word per paper), paper-clipped together, and turned into the instructor.

Step 8: Each group will pick a stack of clues randomly from those turned in by other groups. Each group then attempts to pick out the correct painting associated with these key words.

*Once all the groups have located the corresponding paintings, each student will have their picture taken while looking through the face-shaped hole in their group's painting. This picture will be included in the final portfolio, along with the written reflections.*

Step 9: Each group (A) will locate the group (B) whose clues they received. Group B will explain their article/key words in depth to Group A. Group A will then explain their article/key words to Group C.

Step 10: Written reflection: (1 page in English due the following day): What did you learn about the person(s) depicted in the other group's article? What are the differences between the textbook and this article in terms of Sami representation?

*Photo courtesy of Troms fylkeskommune*

**Inga Juuso fortalte mye interessant om den samiske joiketradisjonen.**

### Joikedialekter

Det finnes fire joikedialekter i den samiske kulturen, Nordsamisk, Sørsamisk, Lulesamisk og Skoltesamisk (øst). Nordsamisk joiketradisjon er mest ivaretatt i dag, og er den tradisjonen Inga tilhører. Joikene kan også blandes med både arabisk sang, flamenco og indiansk sang.

### Hva slags elementer finner vi i joiker?

Tradisjonelt finnes det fire hoved-joikeelementer: Person-joiker, dyre-joiker, naturjoiker og rituelle joiker. Naturjoiker beskriver for eksempel et fjell, en stein, et fiskevann man er glad i eller et sted som betyr noe spesielt for deg.

I. Turn to your neighbor and describe what you see in this picture.

II. Svar pa spørsmålene nederst:

    A.   Hva heter artisten?

    B.   Hva slags dialeketer er i joik tradisjonen?

    C.   Hvilke elementer er mest brukt i joik?

---

## Sametinget

Sametingets 39 representater samles fire ganger i året til ting i Karasjok. Samer fra hele landet er representert.

### Sametingets medlemmer 1993-97

Sametinget møtes fire ganger i året, mens Sametingsrådet møtes hver måned. Sametingsrådet har følgende sammensetning:

President: Ole Henrik Magga

Visepresident: Ing-Lill Pavall

Medlemmer: Jarle Jonassen, Maret Guhttor og Alf Nystad

*Photo courtesy of Sametinget, Sweden*

I. Turn to your neighbor and describe what you see in this picture.

II. Svar spørsmålene nederst:

    A.   Hva heter presidenten av Sametingsrådet?

    B.   Når/Hvor møter Sametinget?

    C.   Når/Hvor møter Sametingsrådet?

Example 3: True Crime (Polish, upper intermediate)

You've already seen the two components of this unit in Chapter One and Chapter Four. These materials were developed some years ago by Ania Franczak, Czesia Kolak, and myself, at a workshop organized by the University of Hawai'i at Mānoa's National Foreign Language Resource Center. It's worth briefly discussing the whole unit here to show how the two parts complement one another.

We used two rather disparate texts about aspects of crime. The first is the magazine article "Like A Stone Into Water," the text about disappearances that we looked at in Chapter One. The second is the video clip about a robbery and murder at a train station that was discussed in Chapter Four. The packet is aimed at intermediate to upper intermediate learners of Polish.

As we developed the materials we tried to follow the advice given throughout this book. Much of the important language from the first text reappears in the second text, though the second one takes a slightly different focus. Both texts include information about contemporary Poland, while they concern topics that are somewhat familiar from American popular culture. The sequencing moves from receptive skills (reading and viewing) to productive skills (speaking and writing). All four skills are involved, though because of the focus of the workshop in which they were developed, there is an emphasis on the receptive skills—as I mentioned earlier, if we were to do these materials over again we'd include more speaking and writing tasks. Throughout the materials we tried to keep the tasks interactive by requiring students to actively speculate, predict, and infer, rather than feeding them information and language.

# Resources

There are no books that I am aware of dealing exclusively with the creation of integrated skills packets, though many published language learning coursebooks claim (with varying degrees of veracity) to take an "integrated skills" approach. Some methods guides devote a chapter or so to the topic, including the following book:

> McDonough, J., & Shaw, C. (2003). *Materials and methods in ELT: A teacher's guide (2nd ed.).* Oxford: Blackwell.

Otherwise, I recommend the books on materials development already mentioned in Chapter One:

> Byrd, P. (Ed.). (1994). *Material writer's guide.* New York: Heinle & Heinle.

> Larimer, R. E., & Schleicher, L. (Eds.). (1999). *New ways in using authentic materials in the classroom.* Alexandria, VA: TESOL.

> Tomlinson, B. (Ed.). (1998). *Materials development in language teaching.* Cambridge: Cambridge University Press.

It's worth repeating that the ideas behind what I have called integrated skills are the same as those underlying content-based approaches to language teaching, which have been widely adopted in ESL teaching in K-12 settings in the United States. Content-based language instruction argues convincingly that language should be taught through content, with the latter always center stage. This is the approach I have been arguing for throughout this book. If you're interested in reading more about this fascinating approach to language learning, I recommend the following books:

Brinton, D. M., & Master, P. (1997). *New ways in content-based instruction*. Alexandria, VA: TESOL.

Brinton, D. M., Wesche, M., & Snow, M. A. (2003). *Content-based second language instruction*. Ann Arbor: University of Michigan Press.

Haley, M. H., & Austin, T. Y. (2003). *Content-based second language teaching and learning: An interactive approach*. New York: Allyn & Bacon.

Snow, M. A., & Brinton, D. M. (Eds.) (1997). *The content-based classroom: Perspectives on integrating language and content*. New York: Longman.

Stryker, S. B., & Leaver, B. L. (1997). *Content-based instruction in foreign language education: Models and methods*. Washington, DC: Georgetown University Press.

Finally, an excellent web-based introduction to content-based intruction, together with a more detailed reading list, is provided by CoBaLTT (Content-Based Language Teaching Using Technology), a project of CARLA, the Title VI National Resource Center at the University of Minnesota. It can be found at the following web address: http://www.carla.umn.edu/cobaltt/cbi.html

# Appendix I
# Using Technology to Develop Materials
### *by Louis Janus*

## What We Mean by Technology

Technology can cover a huge area, ranging from computer use to audio and video production, to word-processing. We will define 'technology' broadly as everything beyond paper and books, beyond the use of here-and-now presentations or demonstrations. All who have either used technology in teaching, or who are aware of current trends, know that changes in technology come at an alarmingly fast rate. If you start developing a project intending to use the "latest and greatest" computer program, you may have to change to other programs more than once before you've completed it. A larger project should not be begun without considering your goals, available time, and frustration tolerance.

On a recent discussion on the mailing list FL-TEACH, one teacher commented, quite correctly in our opinion, that technology should enhance the curriculum, not dictate it. At the outset of planning for using technology, I want to remind classroom teachers that there is nothing that can trump a compelling classroom presentation or discussion. A fancy and glitzy computer-based exercise will not improve a poorly conceived pedagogical approach. Since language use (and learning) involves human-to-human communication, this is a logical place to start. Human teachers can see on their students' faces how well the points are being understood. A student can ask for more explanation, or get immediate (and helpful feedback) to an answer or exercise. The most sophisticated use of any kind of technology will never come close to these interpersonal relationships. However, we all know there are some aspects of learning a second language that can benefit from repetition and from using a delivery system that allows students to access material from outside of a formal classroom— anywhere, anytime. These kinds of benefits encourage us teachers to venture out into the world of technology, but we should never forget the real reasons for learning and using another language.

Using modern technology to bring authentic sights, sounds, and texts to our students' desktops gives us as LCTL teachers an incredible opportunity to make our languages real, living, and exciting parts of our students' lives. Integrating the several modalities discussed elsewhere in this book into a single coherent set of lessons using technology is a real advantage. Even the simplest computer lessons can combine, for example, written texts, sounds and graphics. For additional useful tools and teacher-produced presentations, please check this book's supplementary web pages at: http://carla.umn.edu/lctl/development.

## Tour of Some Useful Tools

We will take a sightseeing tour of some tools that teachers can use to create materials and lessons for their LCTL classrooms. We cannot consider every single tool, but will point out some of the more useful tools and discuss their relative merits. The teacher (in consultation with others, such as media center staff and other teachers) will want to consider relative advantages and disadvantages of creating material using technology, and also which tool serves the purpose most effectively.

Generally, the simpler the creation tool, the less flexible it is. That is, very simple tools for material creation do one thing, and as a rule can do that one thing very well, but the tool typically does not have the flexibility to change the output or structure.

As examples of simple-to-use software tools, PowerPoint and Keynote serve a valuable function for teachers who wish to create effective explanations quickly and efficiently. These are easily developed, and can be shown during class periods and then shared with students for review. As general purpose tools, their intuitive process for development and delivery of information should not be overlooked by LCTL teachers. Many students in LCTL classes can also develop their own presentations and reviews, and can share them with other class members. However, the scope of these tools is rather limited to presentation creation. One could not, for example, create self-correcting cloze exercises using these tools.

## TrackStar

TrackStar (http://trackstar.4teachers.org/trackstar) provides a very simple tool for teachers to organize and present a web lesson. It assembles and annotates already existing web sites as you direct it. This program helps teachers create an online 'Track': a set of web pages with annotations and questions for students; each Track brings together several 'normal' web pages: pages not created for or by TrackStar. In other words, these web pages constitute raw 'authentic' material meant for native speakers. The creator then writes a guide for each web page. TrackStar sets up a grid (or track) with the target pages' links and the teacher's notes. This track is saved on the TrackStar server, and teachers can then give the URL to students. Comments and questions on the TrackStar 'tracks' can even be written by the teacher in non-Latin characters, and if the users' browser allows for these letters, all should work fine.

Carolyn Coote, an Italian teacher at a middle school in Australia, uses Trackstar to bring her students to a variety of webpages, including games, the BBC's Italian phrase page and audio discussions in Italian, and the Internet Picture Dictionary with flashcards of the names animals in Italian, among

*Screenshot found at: http://trackstar.4teachers.org/trackstar/ts/viewTrackMembersFrames.do?number=256354&password=*

other sites. Notice in the illustration below how the selected web pages Ms. Coote wants her students to visit are listed (and clickable) on the left side of the track's window. For each webpage, as in the one below, her comments are in a frame on the top.

Trackstar's documentation is excellent, and its intuitive design makes it simple for the teacher to jump right in and create a track or two. The process is easy, and the results look professional. Your students can use the tracks right away.

The next screenshot shows the basic webform for creating a new track. To start a new track, you should select a few webpages, and note their URLs. (Cutting and pasting from a list would save you the trouble of re-typing when you are asked to enter the web pages' addresses.) To create a track, you have to register on the homepage (with your email address, no cost), and make several selections on

*Screenshot found at: http://trackstar.4teachers.org/trackstar/mts/startTrack.do?submit=Make+New+Track*

topics and levels. After you have created your materials using Trackstar, keep in mind that the pages you have guided your students to might change or disappear over time. Checking occasionally is necessary.

An additional service of Trackstar is QuizStar, an online resource to create and manage online quizzes for your students. It is available only to K-12 teachers, is free, and offers quizzes for the students and record-keeping assistance for the teachers (http://quizstar.4teachers.org). Rubistar helps teachers create evaluation rubrics to score students' extended written or oral responses (http://rubistar.4teachers.org). Finally, Web Worksheet Wizard allows teachers to create and publish lessons, worksheets, and class pages (http://wizard.4teachers.org). Project Poster allows students in registered classes to make school projects and short reports quickly and easily, and post them on the Internet (http://wizard.4teachers.org).

## WebQuest

WebQuest provides another approach to focusing students' activities as they search out information on websites. WebQuest describes itself as an

> inquiry-oriented activity in which most or all of the information used by learners is drawn from the Web. WebQuests are designed to use learners' time well, to focus on using information rather than looking for it, and to support learners' thinking at the levels of analysis, synthesis and evaluation.[1]

Each Webquest includes a standard set of organizing topics, including Introduction, Task, Process, Evaluation, Conclusion, Teacher Page, and Credits. Teachers interested in developing Webquests for their students can use a template from the website at: http://webquest.sdsu.edu/LessonTemplate. html. In addition, the Webquest design page provides a step-by-step plan for creating webquests, with links for explaining each step (http://webquest.sdsu.edu/designsteps /index.html).

## Makers

Our sightseeing tour now heads to tools that help teachers organize and create new presentations and quizzing exercises. "Makers" is a set of creation tools for language teachers. The teachers fill out specific forms on the web, press the 'create' exercise button (with various names), and the exercise is created using Java script and other programming resources. The html code (the code that displays the information using a browser) and Javascript code (the code that evaluates the answers) are generated automatically, and the page is immediately usable by language students from a temporary server. Nevertheless it is recommended that teachers move their exercises to their own local and more permanent webserver.

While Makers are fairly old (by technology standards), most continue to work, but some types of exercises are limited now to certain browsers and platforms. So before going too far in exercise development, it makes sense to test a sample using several browsers and operating systems that your audience is most likely to use.

Makers can create a variety of types of exercises. GlossMaker (http://elsiesgi.cla.umn.edu/gloss/ glossmaker.htm) provides a simple way to allow students to click on specific words in a text and see

> Vet du hva ukedagene heter på norsk?
>
> mandag, tirsda= C , onsdag. t=rsdag C , fredag, *lørdag* C , søndag
>
> Show Answers    Clear Answers

---

1       http://webquest.sdsu.edu/overview.htm

the gloss. Clozemaker (http://elsiesgi.cla.umn.edu/cloze/clozemaker.htm) creates cloze exercises in which students fill out words in a context. EvalMaker (http://elsiesgi.cla.umn.edu/eval/evalmaker.htm) allows teachers to create questions and make suggestions of correct answers; students then compare their answer to the suggested one. MatchMaker (http://elsiesgi.cla.umn.edu/match/matchmaker.htm) allows students to match items in two columns, and reports on the correctness of the choices. MultiMaker (http://elsiesgi.cla.umn.edu/multi/multimaker.htm) creates multiple choice questions and gives instant feedback, which can give specific reasons why the selection was or was not correct.

All of the Makers allow non-Latin characters, with a special version available for a few Makers for material in CJK languages (Chinese, Japanese and Korean). In general if your operating system can generate these characters, Makers can include them in the students' version of the exercises.

## COMET

At the time of this writing, COMET, a new set of easy-to-use templates, is under development by Yale University's Center for Language Studies. These templates will have a uniform and easy to use interface for teachers who want to develop instructional material for LCTLs. The nine modules under development include glossary creation and support, video clip display with support student viewing, an easy-to-create gallery of images and sounds for flashcard development, listening support which will allow students to toggle between the standard language and regional varieties of the same text, support for students' note-taking as they watch video clips or listen to audio clips, dictation material creation, grammar exercises, and explanations of grammar concepts. Current details about COMET's development is available from: http://comet.cls.yale.edu.

## Hot Potatoes

The next level up in terms of complexity is Hot Potatoes, a package of exercise creation programs from Half-Baked Software, Inc. (http://hotpot.uvic.ca).

The Hot Potatoes suite includes six applications, enabling you to create interactive multiple-choice, short-answer, jumbled-sentence, crossword, matching/ordering and gap-fill exercises for the World Wide Web.

In contrast to Makers, where the developer adds content directly on a Web form and the code is generated remotely, creating exercises using Hot Potatoes involves the developer downloading a set of stand-alone programs and creating exercises from the downloaded program. After downloading the program, the developer creates the exercises locally. Once the exercises are created, Hot Potatoes generates the codes (generally three separate, but related files). To make the files accessible around the world or across campus, they must then be served from a web site.

Hot Potatoes' powerful exercise development tools take a bit of up-front familiarization time, and some experimentation, but once beyond that, teachers can probably produce a wide variety of exercises (and types of exercises) with minimal time and effort. The documentation is excellent, available in several languages, and will ease the learning curve. The downloadable package includes tutorials (done in Hot Potatoes, of course) to get the developer up and running in a matter of minutes. For more complex tasks, one can refer to the complete set of explanatory documentation.

Below are several screen shots of a multiple choice exercise I developed using Hot Potatoes in about 10 minutes. They include a link to an audio clip of common Norwegian names, and help students hone their listening skills.

*Hot Potatoes: hint when wrong answer is selected in multiple choice*

*Screen shot of listening activity developed using Hot Potatoes*

## Direct Web Page Writing

Another approach that does not use Hot Potatoes, but creates web pages directly (something that is easier and easier with page creation tools), is shown on the next page, created by Nancy Aarsvold at St. Olaf College. She had previously secured an agreement from the Norwegian radio station that produced these short audio clips.

Aarsvold also wants her students to be more familiar with current events in Norway and to learn vocabulary typically found in news reports. She is trying to make it as easy as possible for teachers to add new clips to the web page shown above by using a blog format, which only takes a few minutes to update. Plans involve doing five 30-60 second clips per week.

## Quia, and FlashCard Exchange

There is a plethora of other tools similar to Makers and Hot Potatoes that are available for designing exercises. Commercial programs like Quia (http://www.quia.com) and non-commercial programs like the Amazing Flash Card Machine (http://www.flashcardmachine.com) or Flashcard Exchange (http://flashcardexchange.com) allow teachers to create online flashcards for students to use. Collections of flash card decks created by others can also prove valuable. As an example, Flash Card

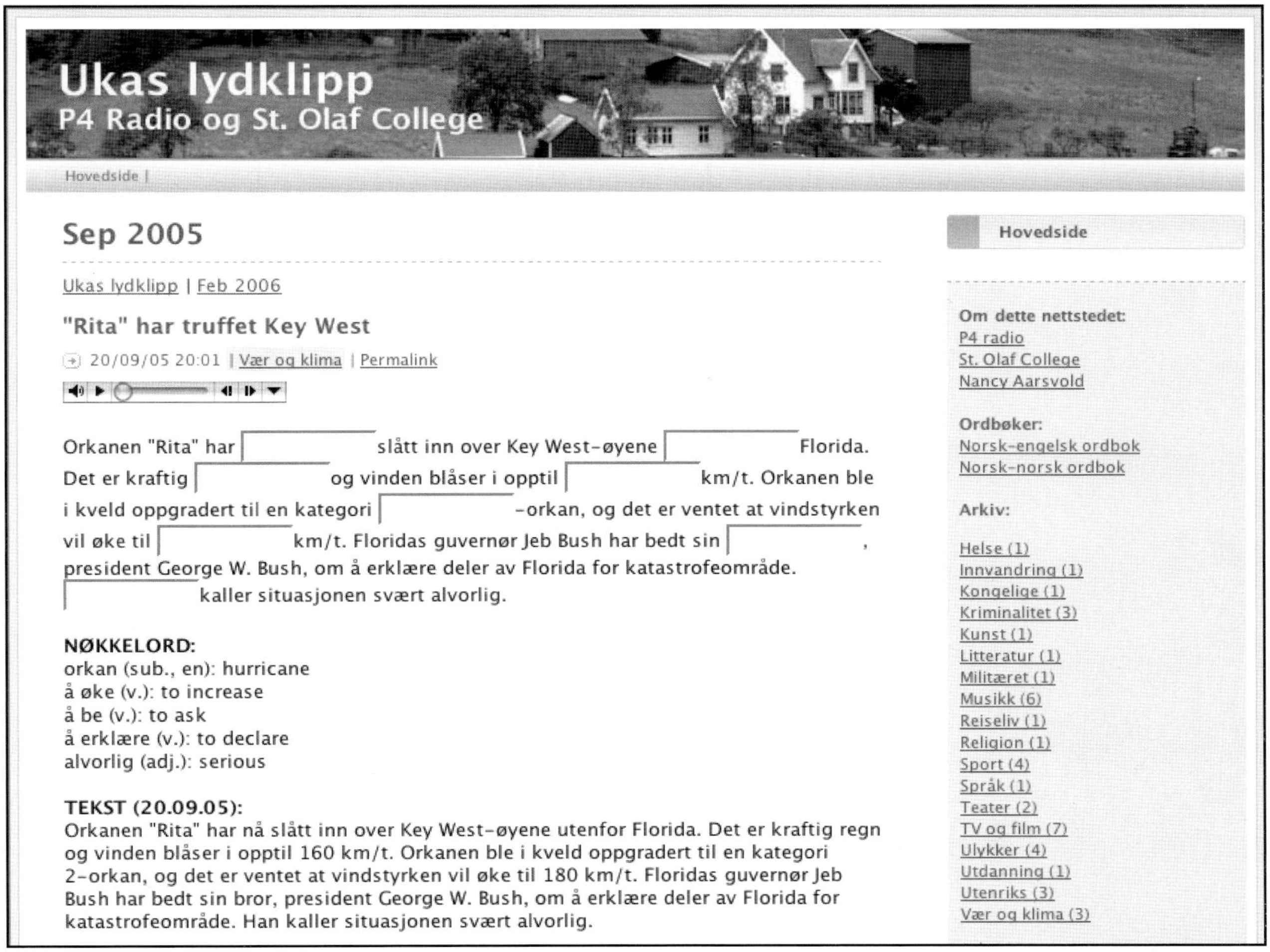

Ukas lydklipp
P4 Radio og St. Olaf College

Hovedside |

Sep 2005

Ukas lydklipp | Feb 2006

"Rita" har truffet Key West

20/09/05 20:01 | Vær og klima | Permalink

Orkanen "Rita" har ____ slått inn over Key West-øyene ____ Florida. Det er kraftig ____ og vinden blåser i opptil ____ km/t. Orkanen ble i kveld oppgradert til en kategori ____ -orkan, og det er ventet at vindstyrken vil øke til ____ km/t. Floridas guvernør Jeb Bush har bedt sin ____, president George W. Bush, om å erklære deler av Florida for katastrofeområde. ____ kaller situasjonen svært alvorlig.

**NØKKELORD:**
orkan (sub., en): hurricane
å øke (v.): to increase
å be (v.): to ask
å erklære (v.): to declare
alvorlig (adj.): serious

**TEKST (20.09.05):**
Orkanen "Rita" har nå slått inn over Key West-øyene utenfor Florida. Det er kraftig regn og vinden blåser i opptil 160 km/t. Orkanen ble i kveld oppgradert til en kategori 2-orkan, og det er ventet at vindstyrken vil øke til 180 km/t. Floridas guvernør Jeb Bush har bedt sin bror, president George W. Bush, om å erklære deler av Florida for katastrofeområde. Han kaller situasjonen svært alvorlig.

Hovedside

Om dette nettstedet:
P4 radio
St. Olaf College
Nancy Aarsvold

Ordbøker:
Norsk-engelsk ordbok
Norsk-norsk ordbok

Arkiv:
Helse (1)
Innvandring (1)
Kongelige (1)
Kriminalitet (3)
Kunst (1)
Litteratur (1)
Militæret (1)
Musikk (6)
Reiseliv (1)
Religion (1)
Sport (4)
Språk (1)
Teater (2)
TV og film (7)
Ulykker (4)
Utdanning (1)
Utenriks (3)
Vær og klima (3)

*Web page created with page creation tools: Norwegian sound clip, with cloze, transcript, key word glossary. Screenshot found at: http://www.norsknett.com/news/files/archive-0.html.*

Exchange currently lists online (or virtual) flashcards in these LCTLs, among others: Arabic, Chinese, Czech, Danish, Dutch, Esperanto, Farsi, Greek (Classical and Modern), Hawaiian, Hebrew, Hindi, Hungarian, Indonesian, Irish, Japanese, Korean, Latin, Norwegian, Portuguese, Russian, Tagalog, Turkish, and Welsh. Viewing and studying these words is free on Flash Card Exchange, but one needs to join for a small amount of money to create new decks, and to print the cards from a deck. A deck of cards, once created, can be used in normal flash card mode (see one side of a card, and flip to the other side), or used in a memory game as a mnemonic device. Other activities provided by Quia include asking students to order a sequence, play several games in which students advance by answering questions correctly, matching, cloze, and a scavenger hunt in which students seek information on specific web pages.

## Finding Raw Material

For teachers designing their own exercises, there are a number of resources for finding free (royalty-free and copyright-free) material. A set of line-drawings representing many areas that LCTL teachers can draw on was developed by Kazumi Hatasa (Department of Foreign Languages and Literatures, Purdue University). This collection states that teachers can "freely use these drawings without any fee as long as they are used for not-for-profit educational purposes."[2] The drawings, available at: http://tell.fll.purdue.edu/JapanProj//FLClipart, are generic—not culturally specific—but clearly illustrate a concept (pronouns, for example) or action. I have used these clear line graphics for summaries of pronouns.

The University of Victoria's Language Teaching Clipart Library (http://web.uvic.ca/hcmc/clipart) offers about "3000 images which...will be useful in the teaching of basic vocabulary in a variety of languages. The characters and objects depicted are as culturally neutral as we could make them." The teacher chooses from among topics like 'animals' or 'prepositions' or performs a keyword search. The graphics are displayed and available for downloading with either a transparent or white background.

*Graphic depicting "Under" courtesy of the Language Teaching Clipart Library at the University of Victoria*

*Graphic depicting "They" courtesy of the Department of Foreign Languages and Literatures at Purdue University*

A number of available collections focus on specific languages or geographic areas. The LCTL project at CARLA, the U.S. Department of Education Title VI National Language Resource Center at the University of Minnesota, offers several collections of photographs in its Virtual Picture Album (http://www.carla.umn.edu/lctl/vpa). These pictures are royalty-free for non-commercial use. At the present, there are several hundred pictures representing the Basque countries, China, India, Ireland, Israel, Japan, Korea, Norway, Poland, Portugal, and Tunisia. In addition, the LCTL project offers sound clips at its virtual Audio-Video Archives (http://www.carla.umn.edu/lctl/vava). Teachers can download and include in their lessons audio clips of Arabic, Chinese, Hebrew, Norwegian, and Polish. Similarly, in the Picture Database at Language Resource and Research Center at the University of Pennsylvania, teachers can search for pictures from Africa, Mexico, and China (http://ccat.sas.upenn.edu/plc/larrc/showpic.html). The REALIA [Rich Electronic Archive for Language Instruction Anywhere] project (http://www.realiaproject.org/index.html) presents photographs from Russia, China, Brazil, and Japan (along with several non-LCTL areas). This project's focus is on pedagogically-useful "materials

*Photo courtesy of the LCTL Project at CARLA*

which convey the everyday life of different cultures." The collections of more than 750 photographs (for the LCTLs) are searchable by language, keyword description, theme (agriculture, folklore, holidays, etc), and location.

Two additional sources of authentic materials for LCTLs are:

- UCLA's Language Materials Project: http://lmp.ucla.edu/Lessons.aspx?menu=003

- Michigan State University's E-LCTL Project: http://www.elctl.msu.edu

In addition to the collections mentioned above which are particularly useful for language teachers, there are many sources of graphics a teacher might find helpful. These sources do not necessarily offer royalty-free or copyright-free material, so one must exercise caution when using the material they provide.

- Google Image: http://www.google.com/imghp?hl=en&tab=wi&q=. As a test I typed in "Chinese signs" and got almost 400,000 graphics returned; "Hebrew signs" found 44,500 pictures.

Teachers often use maps in lessons and exercises:

- Maps from the University of Texas' Perry-Castañeda Library Map Collection: http://www.lib.utexas.edu/maps

Other country or language specific sites include:

- Israel: http://www.jr.co.il/pictures/israel/index.html

- Iran, Persian: http://oznet.net/iran/fralbum.htm

- Maori: http://whakaahua.maori.org.nz

- Indonesia: http://images.umdl.umich.edu/i/indonesian

- South East Asia Images and Texts (SEAiT) from the University of Wisconsin: http://webcat.library.wisc.edu:3200/SEAiT/SEAiTHome.html

- Free School Clipart: http://www.freeschoolclipart.com

A LCTL teaching colleague reports that her subscription to http://www.clipart.com is rather expensive (currently $170/year), but she finds that it is worth the cost, and that finding pictures on the web is more efficient than searching on commercial CD-ROMs.

While this appendix on using technology has barely scratched the surface of tools and approaches available to LCTL teachers, it has, we hope, given ideas of why and how to think about creating material for their classrooms and students. Teachers are encouraged to look around at some simple yet effective ways to develop material, try them, and continue on to more complex tools, always bearing in mind the fact that good teaching might be enhanced by technological tools, but human teachers are the creators of the most effective material for their particular students and environments.

# Appendix II
# Language Teaching Materials and Copyright
### *by Louis Janus*

The issue of copyright comes up every time language teachers gather to discuss teaching and creating materials, and well it should! National and international regulations on the use of copyrighted material are meant to protect the rights of the creators of original material, and in doing this, encourage more people to create materials without the fear that their work will be used or claimed by others.

The classroom teacher needs to understand and abide by copyright regulations in both face-to-face classroom settings, and in distance ed settings where students are potentially around the world; the more widespread the distribution, the more seriously the abuser of copyright protection might be punished or held responsible.

Creative works such as sound and video recordings, web pages, literary texts, music texts and recordings, photographs and drawings are copyrighted in their fixed form (sometimes called 'tangible form'). Ideas or specific processes and methods are not copyrightable, nor are factual lists that have been created without any creative additions protected under copyright. A list of words cannot be copyrighted, but a list of words with pictures, definitions or translations that someone has created would be protectable.

Trying to strike a balance between the need of teachers to carry out their instructional tasks and the rights and privileges maintained by the material's creator can be a delicate and confusing process. We try in this appendix to present and discuss some of the issues, but suggest that it is important to consult experts or attorneys if more than classroom activities will be developed. Most academic institutions provide guidance on using materials others have created and copyrighted. Obtaining permission to use copyrighted material is always the safest bet. Sometimes holders of the copyright are willing to allow free use of their material; often however, an agreement to pay royalties is required. As the creators of published language teaching material, we recognize the importance of not allowing anyone to use all our material without attribution or royalties. As classroom teachers, we often want to use someone else's to give our students a wide range of material.

In the U.S., teachers do have some extra privileges to use protected material to teach in their classrooms because Congress recognized the benefit to the nation to allow such use, but the rights remain limited. It is a very different matter if those same teachers want to share with other teachers the materials they have developed in this way and used in their own classrooms. The doctrine describing educational use of copyrighted material is known as "Fair Use" and stems from the U.S. Copyright Act, 17. U.S. Code, Section 107 "Limitations of Exclusive Rights, Fair Use." Partial exemptions are made under certain conditions for teaching, scholarship and research. The conditions are discussed by the U.S. Copyright Office at: http://www.copyright.gov/fls/fl102.html and summarized below.

There are four factors that need to be considered in deciding whether or not using copyrighted material falls under allowable "fair use" (i.e., exemption from copyright):

1. Purpose and character of the use;

2. Nature of the copyrighted work;

3. Amount and substantiality of the portion used; and

4. Effect on potential market for or value of the work.

An interactive tool, available from: http://www.lib.umn.edu/copyright/checklist.phtml, will help you determine whether you can claim "fair use." Here, you are asked specific questions about each of the factors which are also explained in detail. This site, from the University of Minnesota Libraries, returns an email or web page summarizing how the four factors favor or weigh against fair use.

A separate part of federal law considers use of copyrighted material for distance education courses, distributed by accredited, non-profit educational institutions. The TEACH Act (Technology, Education, and Copyright Harmonization Act) allows distribution of copyrighted digital material to class participants under certain specified conditions. Students must be made aware of the copyright, and the material being distributed must be limited in scope (for example, not whole textbooks, only available to registered students for a limited time). A full description and analysis of the TEACH Act, written by Kenneth D. Crews, Manager of the Copyright Management Center at Indiana University School of Law-Indianapolis, can be read at: http://www.copyright.iupui.edu/teach_summary.htm.

Since we as LCTL teachers not only use copyrighted material for our own classrooms, but may create teaching materials that may be useful in others' classrooms as well, we also consider how copyright protects our own rights to the materials we have created. Can others take our materials and use them without our permission? Works which you create are automatically copyrighted when they are fixed in a tangible form (like a printed page, a word-processed file, a web page, an audio or video recording). You can attach a copyright notice on the material (most often a © followed by the year of creation) but even without such an explicit copyright notice, a work fixed in tangible form is considered copyrighted, and the copyright holder has exclusive right to use the material or grant others permission to use the material. Registration with the copyright office is optional, but can be advantageous in documenting copyright and filing infringement suits if someone uses the material without permission. (Forms and a description of the registration process are available from the Copyright Office's site: http://www.copyright.gov/forms). The duration of the copyright protection varies depending on when the material was originally created. Works created now are protected 70 years beyond the life of the author. A chart summarizing the dates when copyrighted materials go into the public domain—that is, are not protected by copyright—is accessible at: http://www.copyright.cornell.edu/training/Hirtle_Public_Domain.htm.

Some people who create teaching material do not mind if others use their creative work, and in such cases the 'all rights reserved' of normal copyright doesn't give the full story on allowable use. Creative Commons (http://creativecommons.org) offers copyright holders the opportunity to assign to their works levels of allowable use of the material. The most open level requires only that the person using another's works give attribution (that is, indicate that you created the material). Non-commercial use means people are disallowed from making money from the original work you created, but all educational and non-profit use is allowed. The next level limits the use of a creative work to its form as it was originally produced, not allowing any alternations or transformations. "Share alike" requires that anyone who uses the original in any way needs to allow the same sharing of the newer work. The copyright owner is free to select any combination of these options, and can then use the appropriate symbols that Creative Commons has developed. We strongly recommend that you use Creative Commons to provide clear guidelines to others when they would like to use your material.

Denver Language School
Chinese Program Properties
451 Newport Street
Denver, CO 80220